The Beatles' 50 Most Memorable Moments

By Casey Piotrowski

The Beatles' 50 Most Memorable Moments
ISBN 9781926837291
© 2013 Griffin Media/Casey Piotrowski

All rights reserved under article two of the Berne Copyright Convention (1971).
Published by Griffin Media
http://www.cgpublishing.com

Cover: Sherrie Muzak
Layout: Matthew Heimbecker

Printed in the USA.

ACKNOWLEDGEMENTS

To Kristofer Englehardt for his unselfishness in helping me get this book published.
(Get his books "The Beatles Undercover" and "The Beatles Further Undercover." They're essential.)

To Rob Godwin and everyone at Collector's Guide Publishing. Thank you.
(Get all their books, too.)

To Rob Rodriguez for all he did to make this possible.

To German Sanchez for giving me the idea to become an author in the first place.

To Jay Donovan...without him, I wouldn't be an author...or anything else.

To Chris, Bob and Rob...thicker than water, always.

To Lia Romero for being absolutely tireless in promoting this book.

To Ed, Gil and Ron, my three brothers from different mothers.

To Jim Trawicki and Lisanne Donohue for all their time, energy, support and knowledge on The Beatles Show.

To the guy directing this thing.

To everyone who walks my walk.

To all my animals. Such great love, so little expectation.

And, above all, to the last great American blonde.

DEDICATION

With apologies to the Shirelles...

This is dedicated to the one I love.

Casey Piotrowski
2013 BC

INTRODUCING
THE BEATLES' 50 MOST MEMORABLE MOMENTS

Trying to choose 50 Most Memorable Moments of The Beatles was like trying to find the 50 most beautiful snowflakes in a blizzard. There have been so many things worth remembering in terms of the group's music...of course...their accomplishments, the influence on so many areas of our lives far afield from the entertainment industry and, certainly, their own personal lives, too.

So, why did we do it? Well, it started near the end of 2006, beginning of 2007. The actual 50th anniversary of the band's beginning was coming up...when John...after seeing Elvis sing "Heartbreak Hotel", fell in love with rock and roll and began to hound his Aunt Mimi to buy him a guitar. Within a few months...March of '57 John brought in a school chum and, later, Apple exec, Pete Shotton began playing as a group called the Blackjacks.

Well, I knew that was really a monumental event and had to be acknowledged...celebrated and so we did. By we, I mean *The Beatles Show*...a nationally syndicated radio series that I host...and write...and produce and have been doing so for more than a decade.

Back then, it was a little more fly by night. I knew this had to be great stuff but, the day before I was supposed to tape it, I hadn't written the first show. I got myself in gear and finished that and all the other seven episodes within just a few weeks. (The arc of shows also required that a lot of special audio be produced, too. A ton of work, but, ultimately easily worth it.)

We didn't just want it to be the telling of The Beatles' story. I mean, how many times has that been done? And that's not the way the series works. We don't do what everyone else has done. Somehow, I got the idea...50 years, 50 events...moments. Then, I had the idea to rank them from 50 to 1...in order of what we perceived to be their importance. And play them back like a countdown...a staple of the Top 40 radio stations that The Beatles' music dominated for 3 decades.

Well, I sat down and in just a matter of minutes, really, as I remember it, came up with about 70 of the most unforgettable things, people and events we think of when we think of The Beatles...and, for some of us, that's pretty often. So, I had quickly created a working list without ever thinking about what got those things on there.

So, finally, after I had everything pared down, I asked myself, "What constitutes a 'memorable moment?'". The Beatles have done so much in so many areas for so long. It wasn't an easy question to answer. Landmark creative achievements? Of course. Staggering accomplishments on the charts? Well, that's a factor. Unmatchable sales figures? That counts, too. Things that happened in their personal lives. Part of the story. If it was a real big part of the story, then, it's in. There was no one criterion that guaranteed anything a place on our list. Like the Beatles work, there were so many levels to everything we considered that each item had to be judged by itself...overall...for its part in The Beatles' story. Some things made it with one element alone. Some made it with a combination. But, as we got down to it, it became pretty clear as to what were the 50 Most Memorable Moments...and what weren't.

And, though coming up with the list was fairly easy. Put everything where it should be on the list was not. At some point, I brought in the show's Associate Producer, Jim Trawicki to check my logic as I put the list together. Usually, Jim, among the many other things he does for the show, checks my logic...sometimes checks for my logic, which was the case here.

We had a bunch of arguments as to what should go where in the top 50. Loud arguments...even via e-mail. Ultimately, Jim said what he so often had..."It's your show". And so it is. So if you disagree with the choices...and I think part of the beauty of that series of shows...and this book...is that by looking at The Beatles history as a series of snapshots put one on top of another, there will invariably be arguments as to what should have gone where. Great. If you didn't care, you wouldn't be reacting.

And, for this book...really for everything I do regarding The Beatles... their story is more than 1962-70...Even 1957-70. The Beatles...try as they might have...could never get away from one another...We wouldn't let them and, ultimately, they didn't really want to. Their story continues today and will, probably, until we've lost the last of them...hopefully decades and decades from now. In fact, some of the most compelling aspects of their story happened after the band broke up. Unlike their days together, once they went out on their own, we saw their personal struggles, their individual career ups and down and, unfortunately, their infighting turned 'out fighting'...as they took their arguments to the front page that, while they were together, were kept in the studio or backstage. Much more interesting than "Let's put out another #1 single," or "Here's another landmark album"...but that's all there, too. But together, apart or in two's or three's, it is still all one story.

The Beatles have been an amazing influence in my life. They taught me how to write songs...not that I've written any hits. Their music gave me great, unfailing support when life was really pretty terrible. They influenced my ethics, my morals and my beliefs more than my best friends did.

I'm almost embarrassed to say this but there were only three times in my life when I was so emotionally affected by something that my hands shook uncontrollably...when I found out my mom had died, when the woman I love broke up with me...and when I heard that John Lennon had been killed.

These guys were more than four moptops. They said "We all want to change the world" and, by the time they said that, they had already done it...and would do it several times more over the course of their lives.

If we make you remember, reflect on what The Beatles meant as you go through this book, then we've accomplished our purpose.

Italian poet Cesare Pavese wrote something that I think is pretty memorable...only I read a variation on what he really wrote. What I read was "We don't remember minutes. We remember moments. (Pavese apparently said 'days' instead of 'minutes'.)

Through these last 50 years...God, where has the time gone?...The Beatles have given me more than 50 memorable moments...probably thousands more...You too, I would guess.

Well, these are the 50 we think are the most memorable.

May there be 50 more of them as the years go by.

As George Martin said on the cover of 'Hollywood Bowl', thank you John, Paul, George and Ringo.

STURGEON GENERAL'S WARNING

This book contains no soy and was not produced in a facility that also uses milk, wheat, peanuts or tree bark.

GOT TO GET YOU INTO OUR LIST

We considered a lot of the many, many 'moments' that The Beatles have given us; things that we have shared with them through the years. But a list of 50 stops at 50. I mean, you got two feet, you don't wear three socks...generally speaking.

It really is a tribute to The Beatles that they gave us so many of these things for us to ponder. A lot more than 50, but these are some of the other events, achievements, people that came the closest to making our list.

First there were some moments that weren't most memorable... but we couldn't forget them, either.

JACK PAAR (January 3, 1964...5 weeks before 'Sullivan') - Beatlemania on the near horizon. The band's real American primetime debut.

GEORGE'S '74 TOUR OF AMERICA - The first time a Beatle toured the US on his own, but he left his voice and his Beatles songbook at home.

THE BEATLES RE-MASTERS/THE BEATLES ON ITUNES - The last great hurrah of physical music. The Beatles catalog...45 years after the fact...hits the top ten twice in two years.

THE BEATLES INDUCTION INTO THE ROCK AND ROLL HALL OF FAME (1/20/88) -
Leave it to The Beatles to muck up another chance at a reunion and, at the same time, accept the public acknowledgement of the love and respect their peer group has for them. McCartney blew it off because of "business differences". What the hell kind of business differences were more important than that????

In a sadly witty way, George Harrison accepted for the group. "I don't have to say much because I'm the quiet Beatle. It's unfortunate that Paul couldn't be here because he was the one who had the speech in his pocket...We all know why John can't be here and I'm sure he would be...and it's hard to stand here supposedly representing The Beatles...It's what's left I'm afraid...But we all loved him very much and we all love Paul very much." It was one of those moments when you wanted to laugh and cry at the same time...and a lot of us did.

"YESTERDAY...& TODAY'S" 'BUTCHER COVER' - The Beatles gave us covers that were, often times, as well remembered as the records they were protecting. This one is probably better remembered. The band wearing butcher smocks covered in meat, blood and severed doll parts. Easily, the greatest unintentional promotional piece in the history of the music industry.

THE ROYAL COMMAND PERFORMANCE - Whether The Beatles were good or bad that night, Lennon telling the Princess and her friends to 'rattle their jewelry' was worth the price of admission.

TWO VIRGINS - I don't want to hear John and Yoko sing together. And I really don't want to see them naked together...or separately. Recorded before they made love the first time...Thank God, they didn't release an album of that.

THE BEATLES ROCK BAND - The Beatles hit #1 in another chart...this time, video games. The group's music remade in a way even George Martin couldn't explain.

And, with this, producing The Beatles becomes a family business. (Giles Martin unofficially takes over for his father.)

THE WASHINGTON DC CONCERT - February 11th, 1964. The Beatles first US concert. The start of pay per view. (CBS taped the concert. It was shown in theaters around the country a few weeks later.) Whose idea was it to have the band take the stage by walking through the audience??

THE BEATLES MOVIE MEDLEY - Love it or hate it, it was the band's first 'new' track since "I Me Mine". A top ten on both sides of the Atlantic, proving again that regarding The Beatles, even after 12 years, old feelings...like love...die hard...or, really, don't die at all.

THE DECCA AUDITION - Our only chance to hear the band do "Hello Little Girl", "Three Cool Cats", "September In The Rain" and a bunch of other songs we'd never hear them do again. The Beatles as the original 'not ready for prime time players'. (I can understand why Decca said "no". What I can't understand is how they chose the Tremeloes over them.) The yardstick for the band's phenomenal growth over the next 8 months. And it immortalized Dick Rowe (A & R Director for Decca Records at the time...January 1st, 1962...or, at least, immortalized his word..."guitar groups are on the way out". Thank God he didn't work for Fender.

THE BEATLES ANTHOLOGY - A TV mini-series, 3 double CD packages, a book and a 5 DVD set...all #1's for a band 25 years apart. The only band with the stones (bad pun, I admit it) to do something like this, but the only band that deserves it. And if they wouldn't have done it, someone else would have.

BEATLEMANIA - The first Beatles tribute band opened on Broadway (1979). This opened the door for probably dozens of others and started the tribute band industry...which now includes imitators of everyone from Elvis to No Doubt. We'll know the market has been saturated when a 'Lemon Pipers' tribute band hits the road.

Also, the thing that re-united The Beatles. The four of them jointly sued the producers to close down the show (which they were able to do). And, most memorably, in a deposition for that court fight, John Lennon...days before his death...said that The Beatles had agreed to reunite and record new music for a video history of the band. "Real Love", anyone?

ON AIR - LIVE AT THE BBC - VOLUME 2 - This just in...or, should I say, just out. The Beatles never had an album enter the charts at #1 the first week it came out. (In fairness, in those days, nobody did.) This second collection of broadcast material went to #1 within a day after it was announced for pre-order. These mono recordings... selling for twice the price of the other albums in the top ten...were fifty years old. They came from a band that had been broken up for two generations and was half dead. And, yet, the album goes to the top of the charts two months before anybody can get their hands on it.

I just hope you can have a love affair that lasts as long as the one the world has with The Beatles.

BUBBLING UNDER THE BEATLES 50 MOST MEMORABLE MOMENTS

OK, these were moments that were actually on our master list but didn't make the final cut as we got down to 50.

THE BEATLES "LOVE"

The Beatles "Love" album, music from the Cirque De Soleil show, proved again the timelessness of the group's music. George and Giles Martin took The Beatles' recordings, put different pieces of them together...mashed them up is the term...and, while using contemporary techniques, never once compromised the integrity of the music for the sake of trendiness. Quite the contrary, "Love" is a fascinating extension of The Beatles' work. Almost like a sequel to 'Sgt. Pepper' without the band recording one note of new music.

And, even without the heavy advance push that came with 'Anthology' or "Beatles 1", "Love" became an immediate best seller and turned out to be that very rare animal,...an album by a classic rock band that hit the top ten in its first week on the charts...then stayed there.

In fact, it didn't just hit the top ten. It hit #1 (Cashbox). That gave The Beatles 32 #1 albums between here and Great Britain...among various national trades...in 50 years. That's a #1 album about every 18 months for half a century.

"Love" was also the 8th time the band hit #1 (again between here and the UK) since they broke up. What that means is that The Beatles had more albums hit #1 after they broke up than Led Zeppelin or U2 did while they were together. More #1's after they split than Elton John or Michael Jackson or Mariah Carey have had during their entire career...As many as Madonna and Garth Brooks...And one less than the Stones have had in their run as 'the world's greatest rock and roll band'. (You guys might want to re-think that in light of what I just told you.)

Yeah, The Beatles...without working...without caring most of the time...have been more dominant on the charts than just about any of the other champions of the charts.

By doing that, plus giving us new-sounding, if not, in itself, new Beatles' music, and for presenting the band to a new generation of fans, who will, no doubt, have the same reaction as us old generation of fans, The Beatles' "Love" album has to be regarded as one of the group's memorable moments, too.

JOHN'S LAST LIVE PERFORMANCE

Sir Lew Grade was the head of a British media conglomerate that owned, among other things, the publishing rights to virtually all the songs that John and Paul wrote while in The Beatles...and some thereafter. Rights that, honestly, John and Paul wanted to own.

There is a long, long story about why and how Lennon and McCartney lost the ownership of their most prized creative accomplishment...the legendary tunes they wrote together. Ultimately, both Beatles would bear some responsibility for it happening. And Grade did want a good relationship with both men. But, you know how it is. You lose something or someone through your own fault, but there is, at least, a bit of resentment...and blame...thrown at the person who wound up getting it.

Years later (1975), a tribute was held in his honor which was being taped for a TV special that would in both the US & the UK and, surprisingly, John agreed to appear. Honestly, it's probably because Lennon wasn't letting bygones be bygones. His "Rock & Roll" album was just out and it couldn't hurt for him to go on national TV in both countries to plug the singles that were due to come out from it.

At the event, he performed three songs...the first single from "Rock & Roll"..."Stand By Me" (which was cut from the show...and, by now, is long overdue for release, being John's only live version of the song) and what was nearly the second...Little Richard's "Slippin' & Slidin'"... along with a wonderful version of "Imagine" with John alone on stage... singing and playing acoustic guitar. (On stage with him for the first two numbers was a band announced on TV as 'Etc.", but were referred by Lennon as "BOMF"...(Band Of Motherfinders, I guess.) These guys may have really been the ones to deliver Lennon's 'tribute' to Sir Lew. They appeared on stage with masks on the backs of their heads...2 faces.)

Yoko was already pregnant with Sean. He may not have decided it then, but, within months, John would leave music for family. And nobody would have known it at that point, but those few minutes on stage performing for the man who owned his music would be the last time John Lennon would play in front of a live audience.

Whatever the reason that brought John to the live stage for the last time, it is still a very memorable moment indeed.

RINGO'S RECOVERY

The years as a Beatle took their toll on all of them, perhaps most tellingly on Ringo. The break-up of the band left a void that he wound up filling by drinking and using. He would later admit that he virtually lost years of his life to his addiction. But there was one particular evening that it is probably best he did not remember. The morning after, Ringo woke up to find his gorgeous wife beaten and bloodied.

For every addict, there is a bottom and for Ringo, that, apparently, was his.

He and Barbara entered the Sierra Tucson Alcohol and Drug Rehabilitation Center and through hard work and prayer, Ringo has remained clean ever since...one day at a time.

That would change...perhaps save his life. It allowed him to realize how much he loved...and missed making music. And it began the re-invigoration of his career, which has led to a string of albums as consistently strong as any Beatle has ever given us on his own.

In this case, it was more than preaching about a better life to his audience, Ringo was practicing it too. There is no question here about him leading by example.

More than just a memorable moment, this was a memorable story.

LOVE IN THE OPEN AIR

You may not recognize the title. The song never charted but it was recorded by the George Martin Orchestra and it was part of the music written by Paul McCartney...alone...in 1966 for a film starring Hayley Mills called "The Family Way".

Recorded in early December of that year...long after The Beatles had finished work on "Revolver" and said "goodbye" to the road. And this was what Paul did with his time apart from The Beatles.

John was off in Almeria, Spain, working on a movie rather than his music (although that's where Lennon wrote "Strawberry Fields Forever").

The fact that they were so far apart and that this wasn't a Beatles' project were probably the reasons why Paul took sole writer's credit. But the two of them had long been writing separately, but still shared credits on anything that came from either of them regardless of where the song was written or who'd be recording it. (Considering that, I would love to know why Paul didn't put his partner's name on the music, as Lennon would do a few years later when he wrote "Give Peace A Chance" thousands of miles away from McCartney for what would be his first non-Beatles single.)

Whatever the reason, it was the first time one of The Beatles did musical work on his own. That probably planted some of the first seeds...in Paul's mind...and in the minds of the rest of the band...that they could, indeed, make music without each other.

The first sign of The Beatles' break up. Paul's writing the soundtrack to "The Family Way" is a little known, but very memorable moment, too.

GIVE PEACE A CHANCE

"Give Peace A Chance" was the first time any of The Beatles released a single on his own...John hiding it a little by creating the 'Plastic Ono Band' as a nameplate.

But, nonetheless, it was Lennon venturing away from the band he founded. It was more than the next step after Paul's writing "Love In The Open Air"...It was a stretch long enough to pull a groin.

It also moved towards the message that would become more than his sermon. It would become his gospel. It was also the first of the two universal anthems that would...even decades later...bring Lennon instantly to mind.

It was an uncharacteristic success...basically, the first rap record... or the first rap hit, anyway. Recorded in a hotel room. Acoustic guitars and a tambourine and who knows who singing along, the single still became a top ten in the US, a #2 in England.

But its ultimate purpose, besides preaching peace was to prove to John Lennon that not only did he not need The Beatles to make music. He didn't need them to make hit music.

Ultimately, it was a record that laid the foundation for an end to The Beatles, more than an end to war, ironically. But that is just one of the host of reasons we listed that makes "Give Peace A Chance" one more memorable moment for The Beatles.

GOT TO GET YOU INTO MY LIFE/ROCK & ROLL MUSIC

Passed over as a single for "Yellow Submarine" and "Eleanor Rigby", nevertheless, "Got To Get You Into My Life" was one of the most popular tracks from "Revolver". Probably should have been the single in 1966, but that would have changed history.

Ten years later, EMI decides to package a couple of dozen of The Beatles' best up-tempo songs...starts a whisper campaign that the group might be getting back together again and soon thereafter, "Rock & Roll Music" comes out, races up the charts and just misses becoming a #1 album in America....stopped from the top, as things would happen, by Paul and "Wings At The Speed Of Sound". Still (and still today), no band (other than The Beatles) broken up for more than half a decade would come anywhere near seeing #1, much less getting within a whisper of it.

And, of course, here's where "Got To Get You Into My Life" reenters the story. It became the American single from "Rock & Roll Music" and it just missed getting to #1, too. It wound up hitting #3 and earned The Beatles a gold record. In the process, it matched the Zombies "Time Of The Season" as being the highest charting post-breakup single from any band (although nobody...except, hopefully, the Zombies themselves...knew that).

The song...and the album, would be the group's last major hits on both sides of the Atlantic while all four of them were still alive. And, as all four of their solo careers had peaked, it showed John, Paul, George and Ringo that the group they left, had not.

The Beatles 1976 post-breakup releases are also memorable moments.

THE 'ONE TO ONE' CONCERT

He didn't make it to "Bangladesh", but a year later, at the same venue...Madison Square Garden...John...and Yoko...staged their own benefit. This one for mentally challenged children and they lined up their own list of super names to appear with them including: Stevie Wonder...Roberta Flack...Sha Na Na...OK, they weren't all super names.

But, of course, fans were mainly there to see John, who performed some of his solo hits, tracks from each of his solo albums to date... and the one song...done almost grudgingly, it seemed...from his Beatles' days..."Come Together". The two shows raised more than $1.5 million dollars...$60,000 of that coming from John himself, who bought tickets for the shows to give to volunteer fund raisers. (By the way, that figure was 6 times the gross from the 2 Bangladesh concerts.)

Yes, Yoko wound up doing a couple of songs and Elephant's Memory didn't do Lennon any favors playing back up for him. But it wasn't who was with John on stage. It was that John was on stage that made the evening absolutely unforgettable.

Lennon's performance at the concert would be the basis for his only post-Beatle TV special. It would also become an album 15 years after the fact, and would earn John his third posthumous gold LP. And the concert was also issued on video and DVD, so this piece of history could be remembered by everyone.

John's heart would so often influence his singing and his writing. This time, it would lead him to perform the only fully planned, fully rehearsed concert he would ever do after The Beatles. For that reason, Lennon's shows for "One On One" continue to be a memorable moment, to be sure.

'WE'RE MORE POPULAR THAN JESUS'

Years before singing that he didn't believe in Jesus, John said that his fans didn't believe in Jesus as much as they believed in The Beatles... or, at least, that they weren't as interested in him as they were in the moptops. They were remarks made to a friend, Maureen Cleave, who, unfortunately for Lennon, was also a journalist. She turned the interview into a story, which got printed in Britain, to no great notice.

But, when Datebook Magazine picked it up in America, all hell broke loose. (I guess the pun is intended.) Radio stations banned Beatle records. Fans had bonfires to burn Beatle memorabilia. The band was coming to the US to tour and, suddenly, the people screaming for The Beatles were doing it out of anger, rather than adulation.

There was never a word about threats to The Beatles safety through all this, but, with the KKK, who vowed vengeance, picketing outside of the band's Southern concerts, perhaps those threats only needed to be implied.

Unlike a lot of today's politicians and athletes who find themselves in trouble, John never denied saying what he did. In a press conference in Chicago during the group's last tour, he admitted saying it...admitted saying it clumsily and decried the environment where kids were choosing The Beatles over religion and the whole thing, miraculously, went away.

With society being so much more permissive today than it was in the mid-sixties, it's hard to draw a parallel to something that someone might do today. But, if we look at the Police blotters...sorry, the only thing I could think of...a lot of performers have seen their careers end in a second over an ill considered act.

If the same were to happen to The Beatles today...with cable channels like 'E' and shows like TMZ and sites like Gawker ready to pounce on any celebrity's indiscretion maybe the group would have been sunk. Of course, that's considering anybody would still doubt that The Beatles...to a lot of people...are more popular than Jesus. Or that anybody would care if they were.

For showing that Teflon is one more chemical you can associate with The Beatles, John's 'We're bigger than Jesus' remark is one more memorable moment.

THE MAHARISHI

Though they never preached peace overtly, The Beatles years together, from the middle period on, would be noted for their quest for it...an inner peace, a greater awareness. Drugs were probably the first vehicle they tried and when they found no more enlightenment coming from there, they chose meditation and the guru they'd pursue was the Maharishi Mahesh Yogi, a jolly round bearded man who looked like a mystical Santa Claus, without the red suit.

In February of 1968, all four Beatles went to India to meet and study with him. Ringo left about 2 weeks after arriving...not liking the food. Paul left a couple of weeks after that. He, apparently, had other stuff to do. Ultimately, John and George got disenchanted, as well. Not with meditation as much as with the human being that was promoting it...and himself...which may have been the Maharishi's real purpose in trying to make The Beatles his disciples. (There were rumors of movie and TV deals for the Maharishi in which The Beatles would take part... which...as cameras began filming Lennon and Harrison...became less of a surprise to the 2 remaining Beatles.)

The adventure did turn out to be a learning experience for all four of them. Instead of trying to get 'the answer' from some roly-poly guy who, reportedly, could chase skirts and dollars with the best of them, it's better to make sure you understand the questions and, then, look to yourself to answer them.

The Beatles trip to...and over...the Maharishi is one laughably memorable moment, for sure.

AIN'T SHE SWEET

Near the end of a grueling 535 hours, during 98 nights playing at the Top Ten Club in Hamburg, The Beatles somehow met record producer Bert Kaempfert...who'd had his own major hit with "Wonderland By Night" and he signed the band to a recording and publishing contract.

A few days later, they headed into a studio where they began their recording career...mostly backing British Elvis sound-alike, Tony Sheridan. They recorded a number of songs together..."My Bonnie", "When The Saints Go Marching In" and a Sheridan original called "Why".

But two others featured The Beatles alone. One was "Ain't She Sweet"...later to be a near top ten in the US at the height of Beatlemania, primitive as it sounded. (And it, by the way, would be the closest that Pete Best...Ringo wouldn't join the band for another year and a half... would get to the top ten as Beatle...and as a non-Beatle, too.) And the other was the tasty instrumental, "Cry For A Shadow", the first Beatles composition to be recorded...it being a song written by John and George.

"Ain't She Sweet" is notable because it showed how good the band sounded even in the early Summer of '61. Maybe the best document of the group's growth to that point. Yes, George's guitar sounded like he got it at Woolworth's, but, at that point, I'm sure no guitar company was offering these guys free instruments. You could hear the energy already and you could hear how tight the band had become. (Honestly this track was far stronger than the vast majority of tracks they recorded for their audition for Decca six months later.)

Also, though John was not yet 21, you hear some of the trademark Lennon swagger that was a much a part of John as his British accent... highlighted by that lyric switch in fourth time through when he sings "Ain't <u>that</u> nice".

What we would hear from 1962 through '70, we would start hearing with "Ain't She Sweet". Certainly one more of the group's memorable moments.

THE BEATLES AT THE BEEB

March 8, 1962. The day The Beatles stopped being a local band...or, at this point, just a local band.

That was the day The Beatles...John, Paul, George and Pete at that point...made their debut on national media, appearing on the BBC light programme, "Teenager's Turn" and playing Roy Orbison's "Dream Baby", Chuck Berry's "Memphis, Tennessee" and the Marvelettes' "Please Mr. Postman". Being the group's first time on radio all across the UK meant that the first steps were being taken for The Beatles to move to a bigger stage, from being a local band to a national one.

And, of course, it was the start of The Beatles becoming fixtures on the BBC over the next two plus years. They would perform on the network's shows 52 times, appear as interview guests a couple dozen more and, eventually, even get two of their own series on the 'Beeb'. In the process, they would perform 275 songs...many of which would never be formally recorded by the group at EMI and virtually all of those would become the foundation of "Live At The BBC", which would take the group back to the top of the charts an amazing 30+ years after most of those songs were done.

But beyond that, probably the most important aspect of The Beatles appearances on BBC radio was that it taught them how to deal with their fans in an environment other than a live venue. It helped create each Beatles' persona. And it trained them how to deal with the press, which would be invaluable in dealing with the American and world media when Beatlemania hit less than 2 years later.

Gentlemen, welcome to the big time. The Beatles at the Beeb is another of the group's memorable moments.

RINGO STARR AND HIS ALL STARR BAND

As Ringo got into recovery, he lost much of his obsession for drugs and alcohol, and, instead, rediscovered his obsession for making music. All the other Beatles had fronted concerts...nearly twenty years earlier. Ringo nearly went on the road in the late 70's with "Ringo's Roadside

Attraction"...as they were billed on his "Bad Boy" LP...and who played with him live as part of his 'Ognir Rrats' TV Special.

Well, we had to wait until 1989, but, finally, it was his turn...and ours. The Beatles' drummer would go out on the road with a bunch of friends. He'd do some of his hits. They'd do some of theirs and they'd call this musical revue "Ringo Starr and his All Starr Band".

And he certainly was joined by all stars...Members of the Eagles toured with Ringo. Members of the Band. He went on the road with people from the Who, Cream, the Rascals, Procol Harum, Bad Company, the Guess Who. He would also be joined by Billy Preston and his own son, Zak. People like Bruce Springsteen and Slash would go to the concert, head up on stage and become All Starrs for a night...and for the privilege of saying they played with a Beatle.

The idea worked so well and was received so well that it's become more than a band. It's become a franchise, carrying on years longer than that other well known group that Ringo was a part of.

And through the years, Ringo and his All Starrs have given audiences many a memorable night...and all Beatle fans one more memorable moment.

WINGS

"Ram" proved Paul didn't need a formal band..."McCartney" proved he didn't really need a band at all. But, to play live and, probably, to reconstitute some of the studio environment he had with The Beatles, Paul decided to put together a permanent band. The first Beatle to do so. The only Beatle to do so. However, the word 'permanent' should be used in quotation marks. Every new studio album that came from the 'group' in their ten years together had some sort of change in its lineup.

Honestly and obviously, Wings served as little more than an anonymous group of session men who were there to serve Paul. Virtually none of them contributed a song or sang a lead vocal. And no one who left that band became a headliner on his own. You could have had four standees on stage surrounding McCartney and no one would have noticed. You probably could have had those standees in the studio, too. All that would have meant was that Paul would have had to have played all the instruments, do all the vocals...and he'd already shown he was marvelously capable of doing that.

Still, by the time they got to their last album, "Back To The Egg", Paul had put together a musical combination that could do justice to his best ideas.

But, after that, he decided to do "McCartney II", then "Tug Of War" and with that, the ex-Beatle clipped his Wings and wound up being able to fly just fine on his own.

Still, whether they were essential or not. Whether they contributed anything to Paul's music or not, Wings was probably still necessary...and probably not for artistic reasons.

Honestly, Paul probably needed to put together another band to get his mind off the band he broke apart.

He could have done it without them, but he didn't, so they are part of the story. The fabricated four in back of McCartney...Wings...is still a memorable moment.

RAIN

The first song that ever used tape playing backwards came about, as so much of what The Beatles did...as a blessed accident. The group had finished working on the song. Lennon left the studio with a copy of it on tape. Went home, tried to put the tape on his home recorder and loaded it the wrong way...his being, shall we say, 'chronically impaired' (to use the language of today) may have had something to do with that. As he pressed play, the song came out backwards. He was knocked out by what he heard.

Went back into the studio the next day and told the others and said he wanted the whole song released that way. Well, George Martin brought a little sanity to the process, played around with John's vocal so it would play backwards in the context of the rest of the song playing forwards and made that the coda to the record.

And it was one of the great early examples of how The Beatles could combine the amazingly creative with the amazingly commercial. Even with the druggy vocal from John (slowed down courtesy of verispeed), it still sounded like a hit. (And George Martin again proved his genius at being able to give both The Beatles and their audience what they wanted by giving us just enough of that backwards stuff so that it didn't wear out or become gimmicky after repeated listens.)

It certainly was a breakthrough for the group...really their first foray into serious studio experimentation, limited as it was. And it was a breakthrough for rock music in general, as well.

The Summer Of Love may really have started a summer earlier with a touch of "Rain".

seltaeB ehT rof tnemom elbaromem rehtonA.

THE BEATLES AT SHEA

How could such a legendary concert not make our list? There was something like 10 minutes given over to it in the Anthology video. Well, honestly, it was on there for a long, long time. But, as we kept considering things in the process of writing and recording the shows we did on the '50 Most Memorable Moments' and then again for this book, there was something we left off our list that kept coming up and we knew we had to include it. Then, we had to look for something else to drop. Well, after a good bit of soul searching, 'Shea' became obvious. Yes, Neil Aspinall called it something like "the last great moment of Beatlemania". But, in thinking about things, Candlestick Park was really that...and George alluded to that in the closing minutes of Anthology.

Even if the band did play in front of 70,000 people that night (August 15, 1965) (and it did set a record for a one night gross ($304,000), there were maybe 100,000 people watching them at their '64 Hollywood Bowl between the fans in the seats and the kids in the hills...and a #1 album came out of that.

Now, perhaps because it was New York and the group knew they were going to be filmed, they gave a great performance...most memorably, the 'Lennon going insane' version of "I'm Down". But, The Beatles did give lots of great concerts after Beatlemania overtook

America and the world...technical limitations, the non-stop screaming, and The Beatles' own claims to the contrary aside.

'Shea' was turned into a marvelous, legendary TV special...12 cameras were used...and it set the standards for filmed rock concerts ever since. And the fact that it was filmed probably added to the mystique of the concert...because there was a video record of it.

And it was certainly a majestic moment in the group's reign. A post Sullivan show concert that they seemingly enjoyed playing. And, if this was called "The Beatles 51 Most Memorable Moments", then it would have had a place on our list.

But, hey, The Beatles didn't include "Please Please Me" or 'Strawberry Fields' or "Twist & Shout" on "1" and you forgave them.

At least we included it in the book. Cut us some slack (if McCartney and Nirvana will pardon us).

Now...here comes the countdown.

THE BEATLES 50 MOST MEMORABLE MOMENTS

#50 - 'BEATLES 1'

The #50 Most Memorable Moment for The Beatles...The group's album, "1".

It is not here because it's sold 10 million copies. When I said that The Beatles' commercial successes would be part of the list that, in itself, is misleading. What I meant was their commercial successes that really had a bigger story behind them. After all, if we went only by their chart numbers or sales figures, the list would be made up of nothing but their #1 albums and singles...and, of course, The Beatles' story is so much more than that.

Now this is a great example of how something got on to the Top 50 because of its contribution to The Beatles' legend. The Beatles have had other greatest hits packages. Two of them...'62-'66 and '67-'70...both hit the top of the charts...as "Beatles 1" did and, not to give too much away in advance, neither of those albums made the Top 50. So why this one? Well, for a variety of reasons. First, for an album by a group that had broken up more than 30 years earlier to spend 9 weeks at the top of the charts is amazing enough.

Second, The Beatles routinely knocked other teen idols...generations worth of them, in fact...out of #1. They knocked out Sinatra in 1966..."Yesterday...And Today" dethroning "Strangers In The Night". Elvis a year earlier..."Beatles '65" doing the same to the king's soundtrack for "Roustabout". The Stones..."Help!" doing in "Out Of Our Heads" and The Monkees "...twice..."Headquarters" & "Pieces, Aquarius, Capricorn & Jones, Ltd." giving way to 'Sgt. Pepper' & "Magical Mystery Tour". And then, 35 years later, they do it once again...to then boy group/heartthrobs, the Backstreet Boys. They and their album, "Millennium" chased from the top of the charts by the boy band of boy bands...as usual, the one that started it all. Only, by now, this boy band was twice the age of the group they were dethroning and one member of which was already dead.

Beyond that, it inspired a swarm of copy cat releases...Everybody from the Beach Boys to Elton John to the Eagles to the King himself put out their own career spanning hits packages...with the one from Elvis looking like an unmistakable copy...None of them doing nearly as well. And it showed again...almost 40 years into the game, that The Beatles were still leading the pack.

And, if you want to talk about mythical, "Beatles 1" coming out when it did...late in 2000...and reaching the heights that it did...top of the charts, natch...it became the first album to be #1 in two different weeks, two different months, two different years, two different decades, two different centuries...and two different millennia. And it'll take close to another thousand years for someone to equal The Beatles on that one.

And one more note: I remember hearing Paul talking about he, George and Ringo finding out about "Beatles 1" reaching #1 and how they jumped around in celebration...not unlike what they did...with John nearly 40 years before when they'd gotten word about "Please Please Me" becoming their first chart topper.

An album for the ages...literally. One that comes along once in a millennium...maybe and, certainly an album that lived up to its name..."Beatles 1"...The Beatles 50th Most Memorable Moment.

#49 - YELLOW SUBMARINE (THE FILM)

One sign of real greatness is having the ability to serve as a catalyst for people around being able to show their greatness, too. That was certainly the case with The Beatles. They had nothing to do with the production and writing of "A Hard Day's Night" other than to inspire and star in it. Yet they found a young director, Richard Lester, whose work they liked and he wound up making a classic, innovative movie... which bore The Beatles' name above its title. Same thing with George Martin...a well respected record executive but little known outside the industry before meeting The Beatles. And, though separated by a chasm of two very different generations, The Beatles were paired with their creative soul mate. The Beatles wound up doing musically what no other group had done before in large measure because George Martin did what no other record producer had done before.

And such was the case with "Yellow Submarine". Director George Dunning had already begun using a more avant-garde approach to animation...Ironically, one of his films doing that was called "The Apple". One of the film's screenwriters...Erich Segal...would achieve even greater immediate fame just a couple of years later when he wrote the classic three hanky novel...and later film..."Love Story". Together they, the rest of the production team, including 40 animators and 140 technical artists concocted a visual feast no one could have expected. Even those who loved the sumptuous art of Disney's animated features had to be taken aback. One gorgeous image after another filled the screen. Sometimes classical art would play counterpoint to wild psychedelic images. Background images would move in a way we'd never seen them do before. Soft watercolors clashed with dazzling neons. And, in the middle of it all, there were The Beatles...saving the day as love conquered all. It was the summer of love all over again...this time as a cartoon.

Actually, The Beatles had little to do with it at all...other than contributing their name, their likenesses, a few songs...some of which were leftovers or were done with no real purpose in mind...and a short...very short cameo at the end.

And, it's probably understandable. King Features...the studio that did "Yellow Submarine"...and George Dunning were responsible for The Beatles' cartoon series...39 half hours of cheaply made animation which John Lennon said made The Beatles look like 'the blanking Flintstones'. Lennon didn't use the word, 'blanking', by the way. He was more alliterative, if you know what I mean. So, if we didn't know what to expect from a "Yellow Submarine" animated film, neither did they. Ultimately, they would embrace the movie as it became a cross-generational classic, a vehicle for millions of children to discover The Beatles...including, in fact, two of The Beatles' own kids...George's son, Dhani, and John's youngest son, Sean. And, probably, the McCartney and Starkey kids were brought up on it, too.

As The Beatles music from the Summer of Love changed the musical landscape forever, so this animated tribute to it changed the visual landscape of animation forever as well. It is not so much to think that, with The Beatles' film going so far afield in earning such critical and commercial success; it led more adventurous minds to see what else could be done in an animated media. Ultimately, of course, we would get the alternate animated realities done with the magic of computers..."Toy Story", "Shrek" and the rest...And it's not too much to say that, in some way, for sure, those films and all the others like them owe a nod to "Yellow Submarine" for their existence. (By the way, Director Robert Zemeckis ("Forrest Gump", the "Back To The Future Trilogy") and Disney (Do I have to list their credits??) were working on a computer animated re-make of 'Yellow Sub'. (Disney killed it after another film Zemeckis did for the studio..."Mars Needs Moms" cost $150 million to make and brought in just $6.9 million its opening weekend...while playing in 3,000+ theaters. Free clinics had more customers that weekend. But, last report we read, Zemeckis is still looking to revive the project.)

In "Yellow Submarine", subtly, with The Beatles literally before us... albeit as animated figures...the group saved the world as they preached love. The film did as much as anything for creating (or re-enforcing) the image of The Beatles as saviors. An image they have yet to shake. For good or bad, through all these years after, whenever the world needed a lift, whenever it was in a jam and music was at all involved, it was The Beatles in whole or in part that were called on to bail everybody out. Could it be those gorgeous visuals in "Yellow Submarine" was where we all got that idea?

The "Yellow Submarine" movie. The Beatles 49th Most Memorable Moment.

#48 - 'WINGS OVER AMERICA'

The words to me are still unforgettable. Ringo going to Paul's house in early 1970 when The Beatles were about as fractioned as they were going to be. The Beatles' drummer going there to ask Paul to push back the release of his first solo album so as not to clash with the group's impending "Let It Be". McCartney, apparently, flew into a rage, ordering Starr to leave and, reportedly, saying, among other things, "I'll be bigger than you all".

Well, in fact, Paul McCartney, by any account, did become the most commercially successful of any of The Beatles on his own. By the time his tour hit America...the summer of 1976, he was at the crest of a four year run during which time he had 6 #1 singles and four more that got within a whisker of the top spot. Add to that six #1 albums. So, for a short while, he wound up fulfilling his promise...or his threat...to Ringo and, in fact, he was selling records, if not making them, as good as The Beatles had ten years earlier. Only Elton John was giving him a run at being the 70's greatest pop star and ol' Reg would come up short. McCartney, ten years later, had scaled the heights to the top of the pop world as he had with The Beatles...only, this time, he did it alone.

And his 1976 tour of America was the summit of it.

George Harrison played the U. S. before him...in 1974, but it wound up being comparable to a perfect storm...everything that could go wrong pretty much did. From Harrison's decision to bring Ravi Shankar along with him as an opening act to Harrison's lack of voice resulting from rushing to rehearse for the tour and complete the Dark Horse album that it was meant to promote, to Harrison's own reticence to embrace his Beatle past and do more of his songs from his days with the band...And he changed the lyrics and arrangements of the ones he did do. Compromise was not in Harrison's lexicon...and someone should have bought him a dictionary.

There was a reason why McCartney was always the most chipper, most accessible member of The Beatles. For all his other gifts, Paul McCartney was the master showman...whether he was performing for the press, entertainment executives or fans. He was always quite satisfied with giving the customer what they wanted. His first tour of the States...like the others that followed...was wonderfully staged. A good live band...a horn section in back of them. Each show was well rehearsed and tightly played with spectacular special effects. Paul was no longer playing the same dozen songs each night. On this tour, he was playing the same two dozen...with the same between song patter at each stop. (Yes, on a grand scale, it was contrived...Not 'organic' as John or George would have done, but how many people who were at the Maple Leaf Gardens on May 9th, 1976 would be at the show at the Richfield Coliseum in Ohio the next. And, even if they were, who would notice? And, really, who would care?)

And unlike George, Paul did faithful versions of The Beatles' originals he chose to do...not that there were that many...Only a handful of titles he did with his first band made their way onto the set list for this first tour of America with his second. Again, McCartney was there to 'sell' Wings, but, if he had to use The Beatles to do it, so be it.

The show was so well choreographed that Bob Fosse might have been jealous, but that structure took nothing away from the show's energy. People whose opinion I trust, who saw that tour, maintain...'til today...that "Wings Over America" was the best rock concert they'd ever seen. (I had the chance to see them, but turned the ticket down... blaming Paul for the breakup of the band...The Beatles, I mean. My loss.) The sound system was state of the art so the band could hear what they were playing...and so could the audience, who were not there to scream, but listen...and cheer.

And, moreover, it gave everyone an idea what a mid-70's Beatles concert would have sounded like had the band stayed together. And that was the point. Somewhere inside him. Maybe at the moment. If not, probably not long after, McCartney had to realize that the tidal wave of adulation each night was not for him...at least, not him alone...Certainly it wasn't for Wings. The world wanted to tell The Beatles just how much they still loved them...and McCartney just happened to be the one to come out and get the message.

In one of those amazing pieces of irony that makes their story so rich, the Beatle who broke the band up publicly would be the one who, ultimately, would be the keeper of their flame.

The "Wings Over America" tour. Most Memorable Moment #48.

#47 - LIVE PEACE IN TORONTO

In the 'leap before you look' world of John and Yoko in September of 1969, it probably seemed like a perfectly reasonable thing to do. There was a 'rock and roll revival' show scheduled in Toronto and the event's promoter, John Brower, contacted John to see if he'd like to attend...you know, walk around...hang out. On the bill were some of John's long time favorites...Chuck Berry, Little Richard, Gene Vincent so Lennon jumped at the chance to be there, but added one condition... that he be allowed to perform.

Obviously, John Brower was floored by the counterproposal, but it did create one small problem. Seeing that John was probably not going to include The Beatles in this, he had no band to play with. And, oh yeah, the concert was tomorrow. Reliable Mal Evans got on the phone and quickly was able to get Eric Clapton, Klaus Voorman and Alan White to fly to Toronto with John and Yoko the next day. (George Harrison, apparently, was asked and, probably realizing the folly in the whole thing, turned Lennon down.) John almost blew the whole thing off himself, missing the scheduled flight, but catching a later one. He and the band rehearsed on the plane as it flew across the Atlantic. The party made it to Varsity Stadium, where the revival was being held. John promptly threw up...which he attributed to nerves, but was probably a combination of good sense and reality kicking in, instead. And, bravely, they went on stage.

Calling it haphazard might be putting too positive a spin on it. But, they sloppily made their way through the six songs on which John sang lead...with Lennon, often times, inventing new lyrics because he'd forgotten the ones that were written. The set...even with only half a dozen titles...was really a career spanning performance...featuring a cover The Beatles never formally recorded...Carl Perkins' signature "Blue Suede Shoes"...a couple they did ("Dizzy Miss Lizzie" and "Money")...a Lennon track from his Beatles' days..."Yer Blues"...and Lennon's first two tracks from his solo days..."Give Peace A Chance" & "Cold Turkey"...it was a surprisingly entertaining set...rough as sandpaper, but, like sandpaper, what else would you expect it to be??

But that's not the reason why it's one of The Beatles' 50 Most

Memorable Moments. "Give Peace A Chance" had already come out. The first time one of The Beatles released a single on his own. But, considering that it was done in a motel room rather than a studio and performed by John and Yoko and whoever else happened to be there, rather than a formal band, it could be easy to write that off as a one-time thing.

After all, it was still published as a Lennon and McCartney song... even though Paul probably had no idea the song had been written.

And, though George had already toured with Delaney & Bonnie, he was an anonymous part of their band...probably intentionally so...not a headliner. This was John Lennon fronting a concert alone. The first time any of The Beatles had ever done that and, most significantly, the first time John Lennon had ever played before a live audience with a band other than some genesis of The Beatles.

And, in fact, the music from it would become the first major hit album any of The Beatles would have apart from the rest of the band. A top ten, in fact, going gold to the apparent shock of the executives at Capitol Records who balked at putting it out at all.

All told, this wound up being John's public declaration of independence from The Beatles. And proving how much louder actions speak than words, it said to the thousands of people there in person and the rest of the world on vinyl as a result...unintentionally, no doubt, but in a screamingly obvious way nevertheless, that Lennon would rather perform with a bunch of guys he'd never played with before than work with The Beatles.

Nobody may have been aware of it then...including Lennon...but those steps he took onto the Varsity Stadium stage that night may have been the most significant ones he ever took as he moved away from Paul, George & Ringo.

John's first public performance without The Beatles...chaotic as it might have been...is Most Memorable Moment #47.

#46 - GOT MY MIND SET ON YOU

For a few years in the 80's, The Beatles seemed to be in decline... laughable now, but it was true. John was gone. By mid-decade, Paul had cooled considerably from the incandescence he enjoyed for the previous ten years. Ringo's music had long since been deemed irrelevant...a judgment in retrospect, which was largely unfair.

Even the group itself struggled. Its "20 Greatest Hits" package could only be described as a failure...getting no higher on the national charts than #50. The 20 biggest singles The Beatles had on one album and it couldn't get more than 3/4 of the way up the charts...though eventually...even though it wasn't issued on CD...it would end up selling more than 2 million copies, most of those on cassette.

But the one Beatle who seemed least likely to have success was George Harrison...simply because he stopped caring whether he had any. Years after growing tired of Beatlemaniacs, George had grown tired of the maniacs who ran the record industry. The pushy businessmen who didn't know which end of a guitar to hold and whose only talent was being able to squeeze the last dollar out of the performers they had under contract. Without the shelter of three other Beatles and the group's impregnable shield of love to protect him, George actually had to endure the comments and criticisms of these people who couldn't write or play or sing music...only sell it.

It had been building for a long time...through the late 70's and into the 80's. With each passing album, George was less accessible; less interested in promoting the music he obviously worked hard to craft. It is surprising that that environment didn't sour Harrison creatively, too, but the albums he gave us...one after another...were uniformly terrific. Finally, when it came time to release the last album he owed Warner Brothers..."Gone Troppo"...another fine record...George did virtually nothing to get the album any attention. At that point, with the label not caring about an artist...even a Beatle...at the end of his contract, Warner didn't either, giving the album almost no promotion. The record peaked on the charts at #108...although, looking back, considering how little was done to sell the album, that was really a pretty good chart number.

And, with that, George Harrison pretty much slinked off into the shadows and many people thought we would never hear from The Beatles' lead guitarist again. Well, his sabbatical lasted about five years... just like John's when Lennon chose to be a full time father rather than a full time musician. But, where the announcement of John's return to music brought great anticipation, when word came about George recording a new album, there had to be an air of apprehension. I mean, there was none of the 'event in preparation' excitement that came leading up to John's return. Maybe with good reason.

Rather than celebrating his return...as we had with Lennon, George's comeback was viewed by a lot of us with concern more than skepticism and the questions people were asking themselves were obvious ones: Would George bother to promote the record in an environment where creating a buzz about your music had become as important as creating the music itself? Would Warner Brothers get behind this album in a way it hadn't since they'd signed George? And, lastly, would the music justify getting the support to begin with? After all, for the previous five years, George Harrison had been a gardener, not a musician. How far had his skills as a songwriter and a musician eroded?

Well, all of those fears proved to be unfounded. From the first time you heard it on the radio, "Got My Mind Set On You" said that it was going to #1. The Beatles...alone and together...made a career of making perfect records and "Got My Mind Set On You" may have been the most perfect of all of them.

Absolutely flawless. It took a while to get there...12 weeks on the charts, 5 weeks in the top ten before reaching the crest (unusual for a record to take that long to get to the top, unheard of for The Beatles.) The only record from the band that took longer going from 10 to 1 was "She Loves You"...and there was a good reason for that...It was stuck at #2 in back of "I Want To Hold Your Hand". But records that great usually can't be denied...and this one wasn't going to be denied, either.

Moreover, the record brought George back into the spotlight again...and, this time, he didn't run for cover. He worked the media as well as he worked his guitar. Talking to just about everybody. Appearing almost everywhere. Speaking openly...and fondly...of his time with The Beatles. He had begun re-embracing the 'legend', the 'myth"...something you'll hear us mention throughout this countdown.

And the single was also the beginning of his reclaiming his rightful position among rock's royalty. Though he would not do another solo studio album in his lifetime, he was, it seemed, always on the charts. Two huge albums with the Wilburys. A double live album...and, oh yeah, he actually went back on the road for the first time in a quarter century... and while on stage this time, he ran with, not from, his Beatle past. A second volume of greatest hits. And his work with Paul and Ringo for The Beatles' Anthology and the "Yellow Submarine" re-release. It wouldn't have been surprising to find those gardening tools of his had begun to get a little rusty.

The bottom line is that "Got My Mind Set On You" not only had George making hit music again, it just plain had him making music, period. And it certainly seemed as if he enjoyed being back as much as the world enjoyed having him back.

Just as significantly, it would be the last #1 single that The Beatles... all of them or any of them...would have. And for all the #1 singles they gave us...alone, together, in the US, England or anywhere else in the world, it might have been the most unexpected.

And, in doing that...in showing us all again that you can never write off The Beatles, "Got My Mind Set On You" is The Beatles 46th Most Memorable Moment..

#45 - IT DON'T COME EASY

"Poor Ringo". That's what maybe every fan of The Beatles worldwide had to be thinking as the band broke up. What was he going to do without John, Paul & George? After all, he wasn't as accomplished a singer or a songwriter. And, though a magnificent musician, he was a drummer. Pretty tough, unless you're a metal band, to carry the melody with that instrument.

By the Spring of 1971, John, Paul & George each had huge hit singles. As for Ringo without The Beatles...Well, his first couple of albums on his own...one of standards, the other of down home country...and a rumored, but never issued third release of experimental music done with Maurice Gibb of the Bee Gees...a la George's "Electronic Sounds" had to have people thinking, "What kind of creative judgment does this guy have without the others? Is this what his entire solo career is going to be like?" If the world didn't need The Beatles to get back together, if the music industry didn't, then it sure seemed like Ringo Starr did... and quick.

Those thoughts disappeared with the release of "It Don't Come Easy". Even the people who didn't have their doubts had to be somewhat surprised when they first heard it and had to say, "A single this strong coming from Ringo?" It was a remarkably impressive start to his career making mainstream rock music. Probably the most impressive first solo single from any of The Beatles. Maybe the most impressive first single from anybody. Again, just a perfect record. I mean, can you think of anything you'd want to change in it? Strong melody. Great hooks. Well constructed lyrics that said something. Terrific vocal from Ringo.

And, maybe more surprising than anything was that Ringo wrote it.

Now he'd already begun writing before The Beatles' split. And "Don't Pass Me By" and "Octopuses' Garden" proved that the great gift of melody existed unanimously among The Beatles. And, as strong as those tracks were, "It Don't Come Easy" was a large step above them. So undeniably commercial, that, had The Beatles remained together, it would have been hard to imagine that not becoming a Beatles 'A' side in April of 1971. A song from Ringo fronting a Beatles' single. But it certainly would have deserved it. (And it does make you wonder how much better The Beatles would have been...yes, I said "better"...into the 70's with Ringo bringing songs into the studio that could match or beat those coming from John, Paul and George.)

But, speaking in reality, now, the song established Ringo as an accomplished, successful rock act on his own. And it started a string of consecutive top ten singles for Ringo that would last for more than four years...the longest such streak that any of The Beatles would have on his own. But it was more than just a top ten. The single hit #1 (in Cashbox and Record World)...the first of the four national #1's that Ringo would have in the US. (So much for him being a lightweight on his own.)

Yes, George produced it. Yes, he played on it, too...and Ringo admitted that Harrison helped him finish up the tune. That doesn't take away from the fact that Ringo came up with the tune, the storyline and virtually all of the lyrics. Did anyone disregard Paul's work on "Eleanor Rigby" because George and Ringo tossed in some of the lyrics? Or Lennon's on "Come Together" because that song was almost a melodic Xerox of Chuck Berry's "You Can't Catch Me?" Characteristic of the lack of regard that Ringo has had to deal with for decades...but we'll deal with that later.

"It Don't Come Easy" would serve as the template for delivering the message...peace and love...that Ringo would preach longer and stronger than any of his ex-band mates.

Decades and decades later, he still fervently believed in the ideals of the Summer of Love. To me, that just codifies the whole image thing for The Beatles. These guys were singing from their soul.

So, for bringing Ringo...and his talents...finally to center stage and, in the process, showing everyone that The Beatles, in fact, had four great songwriters...four great hit makers in the band, and for delivering the subliminal message that, as great as The Beatles were, there was a huge vein of talent (Ringo) that hadn't even been considered and, absurd as it sounds, had that The Beatles utilized it as it deserved to be, they may have been greater still, "It Don't Come Easy" is The Beatles 45th Most Memorable Moment.

#44 - THE "RINGO" ALBUM

The Beatles' break-up was probably the saddest split in show business history. Sadder, even, than most show business divorces. Certainly, it meant the end of that terrific band that produced so much great, innovative, always fresh music that consistently turned everyone's head around. But, more than the break-up itself, it was the way The Beatles broke up that had to be most disturbing. These four guys who had gone through the purgatory of anonymity and then the hell of fame together...as great good friends preaching love, disavowing materialism and ego and power...wound up throwing all that out the window in a messy, public, years-long, cockfight over money and pride and position. The Beatles could deal with the whole world, but, ultimately, they couldn't deal with one another. It wasn't as simple as that. A lot of factors led to The Beatles' demise...a list that could, possibly, rival our top 50.

But whatever the reasons, by the end of 1969, The Beatles not only didn't want to be together on stage or in the studio anymore, if you were to believe some of the reports, they didn't want to be together in the same room anymore...maybe even the same zip code.

The clouds started to break in 1972 when The Beatles...really, John, George and Ringo...removed Allen Klein as the head of Apple. Early the next year, John made a call to Paul, admitting that Allen Klein was the wrong man to head Apple. It was a big move for Lennon to admit he was wrong about such a pivotal decision. McCartney must have seen it as such...and understood that it was more than a professional mea culpa, it was a personal one.

After that, John, Paul & George all began working together again... not on making music themselves, but on getting Ringo to make music, specifically, his first album of rock music...and, more than just pushing him to do it, they each offered to help him do it.

Ringo met with Richard Perry, who'd just produced a huge album for Carly Simon..."No Secrets" that contained her legendary duet with Mick Jagger, "You're So Vain" and the two decided to work together. As was the case with Simon, Perry chose to bring in a number of big name performers to work. Ringo and the idea of 'Starr and guest stars' has been in place ever since. Of course, the three biggest stars next to Ringo made good on their offer.

John, Paul & George each wrote songs for the album, sang on it and played on it, too. In fact, Ringo was supported by at least one other member of his old band on seven of the record's ten tracks.

The end result was a terrifically entertaining LP, one that produced three top five singles (Two of them..."Photograph" and "You're Sixteen" became #1's.)...No other Beatles' album, from the group or any member of it, ever did that...And the album itself also went to #1, establishing Ringo as a viable rock album artist in the process.

And, in doing that, The Beatles became the first...and, still, only group where all four of its members had #1 albums on their own.

Now, respected entertainment columnist, Marilyn Beck, wrote in the Spring of 1973 that McCartney...who was unable to come into the US due to a pot bust...somehow snuck into the States to join the other three in recording "I'm The Greatest" and she stood by the story when I questioned her about it while she was on a radio talk show in LA years later. Lennon pretty much admitted that Paul was on the track in his Playboy interview, but the claim has never been officially confirmed. Even if it didn't happen, the "Ringo" album took The Beatles' drummer to heights of success probably not expected and, sadly, never duplicated...commercially, that is. His post recovery work has been uniformly outstanding.

And, even if it was only three Beatles making limited contributions to an album by the fourth, it showed that The Beatles' magic...there, as they say, in the grooves...was instantly obvious and still undiminished.

For being as near to a follow-up to "Abbey Road" as the world would ever get, the "Ringo" album is Beatles' Most Memorable Moment #44.

#43 - BAND ON THE RUN

Like wealth and beauty, talent can be both a blessing and a curse. What's that old joke? Some people strive to be mediocre because, that way, they know they'll always be at their best. Well, Paul McCartney proved himself to be anything but mediocre from the time most of us first heard him and, of course, from The Beatles' middle period on, his work was spectacular. Giving us, seemingly at least one standard on every one of the group's albums. Most of The Beatles' "A" sides from "Yesterday" on were his. McCartney had become the voice and the pen of The Beatles most accessible, most commercially successful work.

So, when his first solo album was released, many people probably expected an album full of nothing but "Let It Be's and "Hey Jude's. Well, fans of The Beatles and, quite possibly, Paul McCartney himself, learned a quick lesson. The reason everybody wrote such great songs for every Beatles album is that nobody had to write all of them.

Even as prolific as he was, Paul didn't have to write more than 6 of 7 of the tracks for one of the band's LP's...if that many.

Now, out on his own, short of doing covers, he had to come up with all the music himself. In short enough time, his own weaknesses... like those of his ex-band mates...were exposed. "McCartney" was about half full of real songs...discounting the instrumentals and obvious jams. "Ram" was terrifically melodic and wonderfully produced, but the songs said nothing, some of them dragging on 2, 3, 4 minutes longer than they should have. "Wildlife" was shockingly devoid of strong material, a band good enough to salvage it, and the discipline to know what songs to record and how to structure and edit them. "Red Rose Speedway" was a throwback to the rock albums of the pre-Beatle days...a strong single to sell the album and nothing much beyond that. And, collectively, those were the criticisms that dogged McCartney's work throughout his solo years.

By the fall of 1973, it was almost 4 strikes and you're out...Paul's work on the verge of being permanently cast as irrelevant. Or, better said, being viewed as a solo version of Three Dog Night or Paul Revere & the Raiders...able to come up with the terrific single but having nothing to offer on a long form work...And this from the man who had the idea for 'Sgt. Pepper'. He was...seriously...looking like becoming a 'pop star' rather than a 'rock star'. In the AOR, post-Woodstock, "Rolling Stone" world of rock music in the early 70's, for an ex- Beatle, that would be quite a step down.

Not only that, but two albums into this streak, there were internal problems within Paul's new band, too. On the eve of flying to Lagos, Nigeria to record their follow-up to "Red Rose Speedway", his lead guitarist and drummer bailed on him. So, with a reputation to salvage and with only 60% of his band to do it, Paul, wife Linda and Denny Laine went ahead with their trip and went to work.

It's amazing how often the solo Beatles came up with their best work when the spotlight was hitting them the hardest. All of them. Lots of examples..."Somewhere In England"...Harrison had to prove to Warner that he could make a great album. "Mind Games"...Lennon had to save his career after "Some Time In New York City". "Ringo"...as we said, he had to show that he was more than the luckiest drummer ever born. "Tug Of War"...what would McCartney do on his first LP after Lennon's death?

But maybe the best example was Paul's "Band On The Run". The album everyone had been expecting him to do from the day he announced the break-up of The Beatles...and the album everybody has been expecting him to do...every time, ever since.

Done short-handed. Only months after finishing his last LP. Discovering they had a virtually unworkable studio waiting for them. Having to deal with being robbed at knifepoint by thieves who stole demos for the album. In other words, conditions that no Beatle would ever have to deal with in the process of making a record. Yet, the album was matchless in terms of his other solo work...and, for that matter, most of the solo work from the other Beatles.

Walking that fine line that he and the rest of his first band pretty much drew, of crafting the instantly accessible pop song with enough musical depth to have legitimate artistic quality, that was true with pretty much every tune on the album. With "Band On The Run", Paul rediscovered his ability to write Beatle-quality melodies...in fact, much of the album sounded like The Beatles.

And, apart from the songs themselves, the structure of the album... the re-appearance of bits of other songs throughout the LP...combining shades of both 'Pepper' and "Abbey Road" both recalled The Beatles' best days and McCartney's own ability to craft a masterwork by himself... when he found enough dedication and self-restraint.

In the months prior, Paul had already re-established himself as a major force in pop music with singles like "My Love" and "Hi Hi Hi". But, "Band On The Run" jet-propelled him to a level pretty much without peer through the rest of the 70's and well into the 80's. The lesser albums he would release thereafter that would still reach the top of the charts owing a goodly portion of their success to "Band On The Run". And, in addition, the album gave him back his credibility as a major force in rock music. Album rock stations were playing his songs again...something that probably didn't happen much with "Uncle Albert/Admiral Halsey" and "Mary Had A Little Lamb".

For echoing The Beatles and showing McCartney's own genius without them, and for sending McCartney off on a decade long ride at the top of the world of contemporary music, "Band On The Run" is The Beatles 43rd most memorable moment.

#42 - IMAGINE

John Lennon's first studio album was brutally, relentlessly, uncompromisingly brilliant. It's ironic that his "Cold Turkey" single nearly a year earlier featured a picture sleeve showing an X-ray of his head, because within about a year, "Plastic Ono Band" served to be almost a brain scan set to music. The prism of human emotions filtered through John's own life experience, the result of some tough duty John and Yoko did working with an unconventional therapist named Dr. Arthur Janov. Many of the images coming from John in psychoanalysis were more surreal, more harrowing than the images we got from him on acid or heroin. Through its rawness, its pain, anger, depression and, yes, even its moments of joy and serenity, it was the most cohesive album any of The Beatles...or all of them...ever gave us. And, though it was hardly the most commercial sounding LP ever to be associated with The Beatles, "Plastic Ono Band" sold well...in fact, getting to #2 here in America on one national chart.

Still, having been part of the creative engine that produced possibly the most accessible pop music ever, John had to know that he couldn't do another album like it. He would refer to its follow-up as 'mother with sugar'..."Mother" being the single from "Plastic Ono Band". The centerpiece of that follow-up would also become the centerpiece of John's career, its title song, 'Imagine". Unique among rock records by becoming a huge hit, a standard and an anthem, all at the same time and all of them long before John's death.

And it showed just how much cachet The Beatles...even individually... had. If anyone else had put out a record whose lyrics included lines like "Imagine no religion" and "Imagine no possessions"...they would have been labeled, by people like Richard Nixon, the first of the right wing name callers, as an atheist or a communist...probably both. But, because it was a ballad...with strings...and because it came from one of The Beatles, no problem.

But anyone that did complain would have missed what John was really saying. He didn't mean that wealth was wrong or religion was bad. If I can be bold enough, what he meant for us was to imagine a world in which God and money weren't the motivation for people going to war. And John was speaking about wars in every sense...beyond the ones where people are using traditional weapons...like guns and bombs. He meant wars that also saw world leaders using weapons like politics, corporate power, discrimination and injustice to oppress the citizens of their country or another.

"Imagine" was one of those instances...and there will be a number of them in our countdown...where, when one of The Beatles did something as a solo artist...it reflected on all the band. "Imagine" cemented Lennon's reputation as a man of peace and, with it, as "Give Peace A Chance" did, tagged all The Beatles as peace activists, though the group virtually never really sang about that while they were together. (Ultimately, though, all The Beatles did become peace activists.)

Of course, the record was huge...both as a single and an album. It hit #1 in Record World. And is probably the highest charting record that dealt with an end to war. The album that carried the same name was an across the board #1...hitting the top in all three major trades...Billboard, Cashbox and Record World. And it showed John that his instincts were right. You don't have to sacrifice commerciality for message...or vice versa...something Lennon would forget when it came time for him to record his next album.

Now, "Imagine", because it is so recognizable, has become sort of an 'all purpose' theme that people use when calling attention to any number of societal problems that need to be addressed and that has given added weight to the song...and to the reputation of John Lennon...and, by association, The Beatles. It is not at all surprising that, when Lennon's face came on screen...via archival video, obviously...to sing "Imagine" at the close of the London Olympics, he got a thunderous cheer from the crowd. It is comforting to know that, as "Imagine" lives on, so will John Lennon.

For what it said about John Lennon and, consequently, about The Beatles and for Lennon finding both a message about how people and nations should treat one another and a medium to deliver it that has connected with generations of people regardless of how much they love The Beatles, "Imagine" ranks as The Beatles 42nd Most Memorable Moment.

#41 -THE BEATLES MID-70'S SOLO CHART SIEGE

It took ten years, but a group of people finally came along to do what John Lennon, Paul McCartney, George Harrison and Ringo Starr had done to the American charts in 1964...Their names were John Lennon, Paul McCartney, George Harrison and Ringo Starr. Acting individually rather than collectively, the four Beatles showed that they could still turn out more hits than anybody. It was a period of about 2 years and 9 months, from the Spring of 1973 'til the end of 1975...when John took his sabbatical from music to raise Sean, and everybody left Apple...that the four of them put an incredible 26 single sides on the charts.

It started quietly enough...with Paul having his first real success in the US with Wings..."Hi Hi Hi" just missing the American Top 5. Then... just weeks later...came "My Love", an across the board #1. That was followed at #1 by George with "Give Me Love"...literally, Harrison dethroning McCartney. The week George's song was leaving the top ten, Paul was replacing it...with "Live & Let Die", which would give McCartney 2 #1's in a row...a first for a solo Beatle. As that record was leaving the top 40...beginning in October, Ringo hit the charts with "Photograph". By late November, that single was at #1 and as it got there, John was near the top 40 with "Mind Games" and Paul was climbing with "Helen Wheels". Ringo's follow up, "You're Sixteen" was 2 weeks away from charting. By the last week in the year, John, Paul and Ringo held down spots 10, 11 and 12 on the Cashbox singles chart. A week later, Paul and Ringo were in the top ten together.

Now into '74. Two weeks after Ringo hit the top with "You're Sixteen", Paul was back with "Jet". By late February, that song and Ringo's "Oh My My" passed each other going from and to the top ten. The "Band On The Run" single was next. Hitting the top ten in May and staying there until the end of June.

That would mark 8 straight months in which The Beatles were in the top ten for at least a week. Something the group would never accomplish when they were together...even at the height of Beatlemania.

"But wait!"...as they say in those 'pocket fisherman' commercials, "there's more". (By the way, regardless of how much you like fishing, who wants to carry a rod and reel around with them in their pocket... You mean to tell me you want to be prepared in case you're in the office in the middle of the work day and get the urge to drive 6 hours to the lake?)

Anyway, more hits would follow in the Fall of '74...starting with John and "Whatever Gets You Through The Night"...another #1. (With that, everybody in the band would have hit the top of the singles charts within the space of 17 months.) Paul came next with "Junior's Farm". A week after that, Ringo was back with "Only You". And a week after that, George returned with "Dark Horse". By the end of '75, Ringo and Paul were in the top ten together...the fourth time in this streak you had two Beatles there at the same time...and every Beatle was a part of one or another of the pairings. But that, believe it or not, isn't the hook. John's "#9 Dream" single had also come out. By mid January, all four of those records were in the top 40 together...really, the top 33. Needless to say, no group has ever had all of its members have records on the charts together...much less all within the sacred grounds of the Top 40. The only other group to have all of its members reach the singles charts at any level as solo artists were the Eagles...if you don't count Bernie Leadon...and Crosby, Stills, Nash and Young.

About being on the charts together, George would hit again with "Ding Dong, Ding Dong" and Ringo would, too, with "No No Song"/"Snookeroo" and Paul hung around the charts when "Junior's Farm" was flipped and "Sally G" took over. Between those eight sides, all four Beatles stayed on the singles charts...together...from mid-November to mid February...three straight months. Needless to say, no other...aw, hell...You know what I'm going to say here.

As for albums, well, it was even more so for the music format that The Beatles helped commercialize and then legitimatize. First The Beatles themselves hit #1 twice with their career spanning "62-66" and "67-70" packages. They were replaced at #1 by McCartney's "Red Rose Speedway" who was replaced himself at #1 by George's "Living In The Material World". For one staggering week in Cashbox, The Beatles had four of the top 5 albums in America. And this wasn't 1964...It was nearly a decade after it.

Later in the year, Ringo would reach the top with his self-named album while John was in the top ten with his "Mind Games" LP and "Band On The Run was hot on its heels. By the first week of 1974, all three of those albums were in the top ten together and that led to an 18 month stretch where there was at least one Beatles album, often more than that...in the American top ten.

And on it went. John would hit #1 with "Walls & Bridges"....meaning that within less than 18 months, each of The Beatles would have a #1 album...and the band itself would have two of them.

In 1975, all four would hit the top ten LP charts again...Ringo first with "Goodnight Vienna", then George with "Dark Horse", then John with "Rock 'n Roll", then Paul with "Venus & Mars" and, finally, George, again, with "Extra Texture".

Excuse me a minute. I'm winded.

Overall, the only way to compare what The Beatles apart did is to put the numbers back to back with The Beatles together. If you take the 2+ years, from February of '73 to the end of '75 and compare them to The Beatles hottest period on the charts...February of 1964 to the end of '66...Here's what you get. The Beatles together had 16 #1 singles. 7 more top tens. The Beatles separately had 9 #1 singles, 7 more top tens.

In terms of albums. The group together had 8 #1 LP's...2 more in the top ten. Apart, they had 8 #1 albums...6 more in the top ten.

No other group of artists ruled both the singles and album charts the way The Beatles...together in the 1960's and no other group of artists ruled both the singles and album charts the way The Beatles... as solo artists...did in the 1970's.

And you have to factor in one more thing. Ten years after Beatlemania, radio stations were using smaller playlists...Playing a top 30 rather than a top 40. There was less room for new music. And, regardless if there was only one Beatle on the record, a new single from one of them was regarded as a new single from all of them. Program Directors might blanche at giving over as much as 25% of their playlist to the former members of one group. So, for stations to make room for

25 singles collectively from the four ex-Beatles in about 33 months says more about the quality of the records than the popularity of the band.

And think about this. Paul only released one single from "Red Rose Speedway", George only released one from "Living In The Material World". John only one from "Mind Games". Let's say each of The Beatles maxed things out. They put out three singles from all of the albums they released during this time...There was certainly enough strong material on all those LP's to merit it...and in the case of "Band On The Run" and "Ringo", because those albums were so big, you probably could have released four singles. That means that, potentially, there were ten more chart records waiting to hit here and it was only The Beatles' restraint... or lack of judgment that kept that from happening.

So, for dominating the charts individually the way no one had other than the four of them together, for showing that Beatlemania... in a different strain...continued undiminished ten years after, for showing both the sales power...and the creative power of The Beatles individually...and for implying just how great The Beatles would have been well into the 70's had they been able to stay together, the 1974 solo siege is The Beatles Most Memorable Moment #41.

#40 - ALL THINGS MUST PASS

There is a little mentioned explanation as to why The Beatles broke up. And it's probably little mentioned because it sounds ridiculous...Too much talent.

Too many people writing too many great songs too often for all of them to find their way onto Beatles' singles or albums. John Lennon even spoke to that in an interview in that period of Beatle limbo... after "Abbey Road" and before Paul announced the group's split. He mentioned that the way to solve things...make every Beatles' album from there on a double LP would be impractical.

Ultimately, there would not be enough space on an album or time in the studio for songs from everybody. And great songs from all The Beatles went unrecorded. And nobody suffered this artistic rejection more than or longer than George Harrison. As the third man in...and being significantly younger...relatively speaking...than John and Paul, Harrison was probably viewed...unconsciously in all likelihood...as a junior partner in the creative team...Paul would even introduce him in their US concerts as "our lead guitarist"...making it sound as if he was working for John and Paul rather than with them. He also started writing later than the two senior Beatles.

But if that put him at a creative disadvantage then he grew as a songwriter, arguably, faster than either Lennon or McCartney. George Martin used to mention how John and Paul got better as songwriters because they used to compete...unconsciously...with one another...as to who would write the better song. What he never mentioned is that George had to compete with both of them and, by the time The Beatles were ready to split, he was at least their equal. And Paul said, after "Abbey Road", that, in fact, George had become the best songwriter in the band. But equal, better or best, Harrison was still limited to one song per side of a Beatles LP...no such limits were put on John or Paul. And, by the time The Beatles went their separate ways, he had a backlog of between 30 and 40 songs.

Even if you never took physics, you have to know that that much pent-up energy...even if it is creative energy will eventually lead to an explosion. The explosion in this case was called "All Things Must Pass"... another marvelous piece of Beatle irony... It was a song The Beatles half-heartedly worked on for "Get Back" that wound up becoming an epitaph to the group... George joined on the cover of the album by three bearded gnomes.

It was an explosion of music...three records. This was a box set of vinyl...not CD's. Certainly, a more explosive sound than we were used to hearing from George...Phil Spector's sledgehammer replacing George Martin's velvet touch as Producer. And, most of all, it was a creative explosion. Two hours of George saying "I told you so" to John and Paul...and, probably, George Martin, too...with a work that covered everything from God to morality to mortality to philosophy to love to nonsense and featured writing, performances, arrangements and production that were uniformly superb.

As he grew as a songwriter during The Beatles' later years, I'd bet that everyone probably expected a great first solo album from George, but there was a majesty to "All Things Must Pass" from the look of the package to the last note on the record that no one could have expected. It said that it was a very important work...and it was. It spent 8 weeks at the top of the charts...no Beatles' solo album stayed at the top longer. And earned George a Grammy nomination for "Album Of The Year". And it is widely regarded today...forty plus years after the fact...as the best post-Beatle release to come from any member of the group.

And it began the most consistent, most entertaining musical career of any of The ex-Beatles. "All Things Must Pass", the breakthrough album from The Beatle who had a hard time getting the others to help with his music, proved that, ultimately, he didn't really need their help at all. The Beatles' 40th Most Memorable Moment.

#39 - MAGICAL MYSTERY TOUR

When Brian Epstein died, The Beatles began dying right along with him. John Lennon later would say how he knew the band's fate was sealed with Brian's passing. In the entertainment industry, with great success comes great freedom...and that includes the freedom to make great mistakes. In the 60's, no one had greater success than The Beatles and, after Epstein's death, they used the considerable freedom that came with it to make their first great mistake...deciding to manage their own career. And the proof of that being their first great mistake came with their second...deciding to do "Magical Mystery Tour".

It was Paul's idea...the film was...in an effort to keep the band working...really keep them together in the weeks after Brian died. On a flight back to England from America, he drew out a pie chart...a circle with some lines segmenting it. He fleshed out a few ideas with Mal Evans...and that was it. His shooting script for a movie The Beatles would make on their own. A fantasy based on a long time bus trip that was really a rolling bar for its passengers.

As Neil Aspinall would later say, "We went out to make a film and nobody had the vaguest idea of what it was all about." Richard Lester, who directed "A Hard Day's Night" and "Help!" also advised The Beatles on "Magical Mystery Tour"...and he said "From the moment they finally decided to make it till the time the first shots were made was only two weeks. It went off totally unprepared and half-cocked."

And, ultimately, it looked it. For the first time since they'd become the darlings of the British press four years earlier, The Beatles got panned. It was a cross between a home movie and an experimental video made by people who'd never done a film before...not, at least, from that side of the camera. It had no real plot and even the individual segments didn't make a whole lot of sense. Worse still, the film was shot in color but was shown on the BBC in black and white and many of the best visuals got lost in the translation.

Surprisingly, the film wasn't even a success among TV viewers...it ranked only as the 25th most watched Christmas program on the BBC that year. And those low ratings, as well as the critical drubbing the film took, cost the band a $1 million deal it had on the table from NBC to air the special in America.

As you might guess, the film worked best when it dealt with The Beatles' music. There, surprisingly, they showed considerable craft in creating a visual soundtrack to accompany their music. And the music, of course, was splendid. There was the requisite hit single, "Hello Goodbye" and classics like "I Am The Walrus" and "Fool On The Hill".

And, again, to show the incredible popularity of the group, nobody in America...for years...had any idea what 'MMT' was all about. (Then again, probably a lot of the people who did see it in England wound up not having any idea either.) But, here in the US, all "Magical Mystery Tour" was a soundtrack album for a film they wouldn't see until the 70's when some bootleg prints made their way around the country. There was a booklet inside the LP...another marvelous package by the way... and it told the story of a film we couldn't see. It didn't matter. The US album (The new songs formed a #1 2 EP set in the UK) was #1 for a couple of months and actually got a Grammy nomination for "Album Of The Year" in 1968.

More than that, "Magical Mystery Tour" was the initial project done by Apple...Apple Films to be precise. The first use of the nameplate that would become first a drainpipe for The Beatles' fortunes, then the overseer of the warehousing of their works and the guardian of their legacy.

And, beyond that, it was the first instance of Paul pushing the other members of the band into doing something. His trying to fill the void... consciously or not...left by Epstein being gone. Instead of the man who discovered them telling them what to do, this was one Beatle telling the others what to do...and the seeds for the band's demise were beginning to be sewn...as John Lennon felt they would.

Neil Aspinall also said, "What we should have been filming, if anything, was all the confusion, because that was the REAL mystery tour." In retrospect, though he didn't know it, Neil was speaking about much more than the filming of that movie. "Magical Mystery Tour". The Beatles 39th Most Memorable Moment.

#38 - ALL THOSE YEARS AGO

This story really has four different segments that involve all four Beatles. It begins with Ringo Starr. In the Fall of 1980, he was working on his album "Can't Fight Lightning". This was the LP where some of his closest friends...including all the ex-Beatles would not only perform with him on the record, but produce him as well. At this point, he is at George's home studio at Friar Park. He records a number of tracks with George on the other side of the glass..."You Belong To Me", the old Jo Stafford classic, "Wrack My Brain", his last major hit and another song from George, this one going unreleased. A tune called "All Those Years Ago". Same melody...same track but with different lyrics.

John's part in the story was, sadly and simply, his murder in December of 1980.

Next, we come to George. He had finished his follow-up to his well received self-named album. He submitted it to his record company, Warner Brothers, but they felt the album was too down tempo, not commercial enough and they refused to release it. Harrison wrote three new songs, which are, in fact, more upbeat, more catchy, and, honestly, more Beatle-esque. For the fourth, he decided to do a tribute to his fallen mentor, John Lennon. But, rather than write a new song, he took Ringo's version of "All Those Years Ago", wrote a new set of lyrics, erased Ringo's vocal and recorded his own singing those new words over it.

Next, we come to Paul McCartney. In early 1981, he was in the studio to cut his first new album since John's death. He had decided to work again with his long time musical counsel, George Martin...the first time since Ringo's "Sentimental Journey" that Sir George would produce an entire album by any member of the band. The album, ultimately to become "Tug Of War", had a theme. Paul would write a group of songs and he and Martin would bring in 'guest stars'...people who could add conceptually to that track. The most obvious example would be Stevie Wonder and his work on "Ebony & Ivory". Well, for one track on the album, a wonderful song called "Wanderlust", Paul felt that the one thing that would make it perfect would be adding George's guitar. He contacted him and, for the first time since they recorded "I Me Mine", Harrison, who probably had the longest standing personal and professional differences with McCartney, agreed to play with him again. In early 1981, Paul came to Friar Park...along with Linda and Denny Laine...and George Martin and Geoff Emerick. No doubt, there was much reflection on their years together and, I wouldn't at all be surprised if a lot of time was spent talking about John. As it turned out, George never worked at all on "Wanderlust". Instead, the McCartney's...and Denny...wound up adding their support, in the form of background vocals to George's recording of "All Those Years Ago". Martin and Emerick added their skills, too.

With the music track already featuring Ringo's drumming, that meant that 3/4's of The Beatles were playing and singing about the one member of the band who couldn't be there.

The result was an obvious #1 though, honestly, "All Those Years Ago", in my opinion, anyway, was, maybe, the eighth strongest choice for a single from the album..."Somewhere In England" being Harrison's most commercial, pop-oriented LP. The album...probably because of the attention the lead single brought to it...put Harrison solidly back into the top ten in both the American and British charts

But, sadly, even after that, George and Paul would not get together to record a Harrison contribution to "Wanderlust". They fell out with each other again and it would be another ten years before the distance between these longtime friends would disappear to the point where they would even consider working together again.

In a sense, "All Those Years Ago" was even more a reunion record than "Free As A Bird"...regardless of the regrettable circumstances in which it came to be recorded...with John's implied presence being demonstrated with every word George sang.

Ultimately, it turned out to be an extremely important record because it put George back at the top of the charts for the first time in eight years and, more importantly, because it gave us three Beatles coming together to remember the fourth...the first time those three members of the band would be in the studio together in more than a decade..and the last time for nearly a decade and a half.

"All Those Years Ago" is The Beatles 38th Most Memorable Moment.

#37 - APPLE

Apple was a wonderful idea that turned into a disaster that, ultimately, turned into a blessing, for The Beatles and for us.

Perhaps, the idea came from the Beach Boys, who started their own Brother record label a year earlier...supposedly, giving the group a greater say; not only in artistic matters, but in the promotion, packaging and releasing of their work.

But, more than likely, the idea for Apple was on The Beatles minds long before "Heroes & Villains"...the first release from Brother.

"Magical Mystery Tour" was 'presented' by Apple Films. And a reference to "The Apple" can even be found on the back cover of the 'Sgt. Pepper' album.

John and Paul...really John...described Apple on the Tonight Show this way:

"Our accountant came up and said, "We've got this amount of money. Do you want to give it to the government or do something with it...So we decided to play businessman for a bit, because we've got to run our own affairs now. So, we got this thing called Apple which is gonna be records, films and electronics which all tie up...so that people who want to make films about...that...don't have to go on their knees in an office begging for a break."

Paul added, "if you wanna do something, normally you have to go to big business, you gotta go to...them, the big people. (John interjects, "Well, you don't even get to them. You can't get through the door because of the color of your shoes.)

Paul continues, "Big companies are so big that if you're little and good, it takes you, like, 60 years to make it. And, so, people miss out on these little, good people, so we're trying to find a few".

And those good intentions served to be little more than paving stones The Beatles would lay on the road to their own personal hell.

The idea of giving an opportunity to talented, but unknown people in all areas of the arts was wonderfully magnanimous, but proved very quickly to be absolutely unrealistic. For a few there is, indeed, no business like show business. For most, though, they have no business being in show business. And, unfortunately, those cursed with a lack of talent are frequently also cursed with a lack of objectivity. By opening up their doors to anyone who had access to a tape recorder, a movie camera or a typewriter, The Beatles opened themselves up to have their time, energy and money drained by every untalented nut job in the world who could get The Beatles' address. There was no way they could bring in enough people to go through the mountains of manuscripts, demos and films that flooded their offices to find the few artists whose work deserved to be offered to the masses. And the thousands of artists who were promised not to have their submissions summarily thrown in the trash, in fact, got a chance to have their unopened packages see the inside of The Beatles' dumpster, too.

They did show they had the same knack for coming up with good singers and songwriters that they had for coming up with good songs. People like James Taylor, Mary Hopkin, who had far more hits in Britain than she did in America, Badfinger...The Beatles' true protégés...and Billy Preston. However, it took Taylor and Preston leaving Apple for other labels before they found success. And other notable work from people like Doris Troy and Jackie Lomax never received the attention it deserved probably because it was on Apple. The Beatles, trying to shine a light on other artists, still generated too much light themselves that left all the people they signed in the shadows with both critics and fans.

But, ultimately, what was going on at the bottom end of things was nothing compared to what was happening on top. Some of the people already on the inside looked at The Beatles as four blank checks. The book, "Apple To The Core" detailed the largess that went on at The Beatles' expense...literally. Office equipment, furnishings, a car.... even money was disappearing...faster than even The Beatles could make it. According to a report on Fox Business, the company was spending about $14,000 a month on food. An equal amount on liquor...No wonder everybody wanted to work there. Free eats, free booze and you were working for The Beatles. There were fears, from John Lennon himself, that The Beatles, still together at that point, and selling more records than ever, would soon be broke.

The drastic situation led to a drastic decision...Allen Klein, who had previously managed the Stones...was brought in to run Apple...over Paul McCartney's objections...the only time that a decision by The Beatles was made by less than a unanimous vote.

That pulled Paul out of the day to day operations of Apple...and set in motion his eventual split from the band. Klein quickly negotiated a new deal with EMI, which gave The Beatles a much higher royalty rate, but which also allowed EMI to repackage the band's work...which led to a series of needless releases like "The Beatles Again" and, eventually, things like "Reel Music" that ranged from redundant to absolutely pretty much worthless.

And Apple would so tie The Beatles to one another that, as the group split, Paul was forced to take the others to court to end their partnership and that was the first of a series of legal actions that kept The Beatles at odds for years, as they struggled, for decades to be free of one another...the creative freedom they achieved by breaking up was blunted by the financial and legal entanglements Apple, seemingly, forever tied them up in.

Ultimately, though, that would be a good thing. Though they wouldn't work together artistically, they still were able to have a united front...through Apple...when they went after people like the producers of "Beatlemania". The fact that they could never completely walk away from one another was probably a factor in them coming together again...resolving their business differences which affected their personal relationships with one another...and those would, ultimately, be resolved, too.

And that, of course, led to things like "The Beatles Anthology", "Love", the Capitol albums packages, "Rock Band", the deal with iTunes and everything that has come along since The Beatles decided to be The Beatles again.

Oddly enough, the Apple cart almost went on...twice...with only three of its wheels. Reportedly, Paul approached John, George and Ringo (probably sometime in 1972) about buying out his 25% in the company. At least that would have kept it in the family.

I remember reading somewhere John saying...sometime during the latter part of the 70's...that he was thinking about selling off his 25% share in Apple. Imagine if he did it that way...The Beatles then would have been Paul, George, Ringo and Gordon...as in Gordon Gekko. Three musical geniuses making decisions about how to deal with the band's creative legacy...joined at the table by some shark who knew only about money...and I don't mean the song the group covered on "With The Beatles".

Apple kept them all from walking away from each other and, eventually, they came to realize just how special what they did was and they knew that, if anyone was going to make decisions about anything to do with The Beatles, there were no better qualified people than those four guys themselves.

A sour apple never turns sweet, but it did in this case. It was some of the reason for them drifting apart and a lot of the reason why it never went so far that they couldn't get back together again. And, by the way, for all the money it lost during the heady and reckless 60's, it has more than made up for it with the hundreds of millions of dollars its produced for the band by becoming the corporate entity it was formed to counter.

Apple is The Beatles 37th Most Memorable Moment.

#36 - OUR WORLD

Shakespeare said, "All the world is a stage" and that was the case, literally for The Beatles on June 25th, 1967. Sometime during the year before, a man named Aubrey Singer at the BBC had an idea...do a TV show which would put together people from all over the world on one program...and do it live. Sounds pretty commonplace now, but it was revolutionary then. At that time, we had just reached the point where there were enough communications satellites floating above us to make it possible. Eighteen countries agreed to make contributions to the program. An additional thirteen agreed to carry it. Translators were lined up to deliver the narration in every language necessary. It was supposed to show life around the world. It featured scenes from a Tokyo subway, an Alberta, Canada ranch and included among all that were those larger than life figures, The Beatles.

Though the program was ten months in the planning, according to George Martin, The Beatles' creative team knew about this only about two weeks before it was to happen and they worked feverishly to come up with a new song. It would be John who had the perfect idea. A message from The Beatles to the world delivered as simply, but vaguely, in as elementary a set of lyrics as possible.

As insurance, George Martin had the band record the basic rhythm track prior to the broadcast, but Paul's bass, Ringo's drums and George's solo...along with a 13 piece orchestra played live...to the world. Martin added snippets of "Greensleeves", Bach and Glenn Miller's "In The Mood"...for which EMI would later have to pay royalties...to the arrangement, along, of course, with "La Marseillaise" at the beginning of the song to give it an international flavor. And a virtual rock and roll hall of fame joined The Beatles in the studio...including Eric Clapton, Mick Jagger, Keith Richard, Keith Moon and Graham Nash.

With 30 seconds to go before hitting the air, George Martin got a phone call...It was the producer saying that he'd lost contact with the studio and that Martin would have to cue everybody. Nothing like a little bit of pressure like that when you're going on in front of the whole world.

Well, of course, it went off flawlessly. John would re-do some of his vocal. Ringo would add the drum roll at the beginning of the song, but, for the most part, what the world heard then is what the world hears now. Another instant #1 for The Beatles.

It is estimated that as many as one out of five people on earth at that time saw it. Adjusted for population growth, that's nearly half again as many people as saw the opening of the London Olympics. That really is astonishing.

With it, The Beatles pioneered the idea of 'new release as an event'...a major contribution to musical artists...or, at least, to their egos and for their promotion.

But, more importantly, "Our World" gave The Beatles the chance to be the first musical artists to, in fact, use the world as a stage...Really, they were the first major artists of any sort to do that...The greatest stars of stage, film, music, radio and, later, TV would hesitate to state their political affiliation, much less their stand on crucial issues of the day. In America, at that time, and throughout much of the world, the most crucial issue of all was Vietnam...and the inexplicable war that America was waging there. By singing about global love, The Beatles took a stand...subtly, but they were doing it while 20% of the globe was watching them.

In the years to come, each would wonder why the world would turn to them...The Beatles...during some sort of crisis. Well, preaching love to everyone on earth...and using TV as the pulpit...just continued the job they'd begun 3 1/2 years earlier. Their explosion in America almost right after JFK's assassination accidentally made them appear as the white knights riding to the rescue.

But their appearance on "Our World" was the first time they actively pursued that role themselves. And, for all of that, the group's appearance on the first global television program ranks as The Beatles' 36th Most Memorable Moment.

#35 - YOKO ONO

Yoko Ono was born in Tokyo in 1933 to a wealthy Japanese family. They moved to New York after World War II, where she would study music at Sarah Lawrence College. She became especially interested in the work of avant garde classical composers like John Cage. Not long after, she would meet another student...from Julliard...who shared her interests. They would marry and move to Manhattan where Yoko, for a time, would actually teach Japanese art and music in the New York City public school system.

Not long after, she began to stage what were called 'happenings', a cross between a performance and a party which would feature poetry and music. Even then, her art was highly conceptualized...sometimes existing only in theory or in her imagination...and you can't get more conceptualized than that.

By the early 60's, she brought her performance art to Carnegie Hall...a programme which would include a toilet flushing throughout. The negative reviews she received didn't stop her. She would travel to England in 1966 and perform what she called "Cut Piece" where members of the audience would come on stage, take a pair of scissors and cut off pieces of her clothing.

Odd as that sounds, it made her the rage of the London Art Community and earned her work an exhibition at the noted Indica Gallery, which was frequented by John Lennon. He admired her work, especially a piece where one would climb a ladder and hold a magnifying glass up to the ceiling to read the word "yes". With that, they met, began spending time together and, soon, had an affair.

Not long after, John's first wife, Cynthia, found them together at the Lennon home. She began divorce proceedings and John and Yoko became constant companions. And I mean 'constant'. She started showing up at Beatles' recording sessions...To that point, they were off limits to everyone...wives, girlfriends, even Brian Epstein. She was not only in the studio, she would comment on their work. "Why do the songs all sound the same?" was one famous critique. She would even follow John into the rest room.

John had long been doing experimental tapes at home, but that's where they stayed. Elements were incorporated into The Beatles' most inventive, yet still accessible work...like "Tomorrow Never Knows" and "I Am The Walrus". With Yoko, those tapes became albums...the first of which, "Two Virgins" featured a full frontal nude picture of the couple on its cover. The primal screams we heard on his "Plastic Ono Band" LP, their unappealing first collaboration of far left politics..."Sometime In New York City" and the nonsensical cacophony he would produce with her at the mike and all the 'happenings' they would now do together had a large percentage of his fans asking "What the heck is he doing?"

Quickly, Yoko was earning a reputation as an oddball home wrecker of limited talent who was making John Lennon crazy. Truth is, John Lennon was probably crazy before he met Yoko. She just gave him permission to be that way in public. Yes, John and Yoko got addicted to heroin, but Lennon had been drinking, using pills, smoking pot and doing acid before he met her. And, though The Beatles broke up once she became a constant, by that time, they were well down that road, anyway.

What she ultimately did was to influence John's work more than he would influence hers...Make his music more far out than he could make hers more far in. Make John's work more ego-centric, self-important and more self-indulgent than it had been, even while he was in The Beatles...at the expense of its viability as art for the masses. And, after all, who cares how brilliant your personal muse may be to you if few others think it's worth anything? Vanity publishers across the country continue to prove that year in and year out.

And, though she alone didn't break up The Beatles, the truth is that her presence...continual as it was...probably added to the stresses already within the band and, after the split, she may have helped to keep them broken up. Reportedly, Paul phoned John during the sessions for "Double Fantasy" and Yoko didn't let the call go through to him.

She continued to see John's years as a Beatle as an adjunct to his solo career, rather than, more correctly, the other way around. And her presence as "unwanted sister-in-law" to at least some of John's three professional brothers had to exacerbate their sometimes difficult relationships ex post facto.

But, all that stated, The Beatles' reunion in the studio would not have happened, not only without her permission, but without her willingness to offer up John's demos to Paul for The Beatles to complete. In fact, she said that she knew how much the world wanted The Beatles back together and she wasn't going to be the one to stand in the way.

And, everything that has come from The Beatles since has come with her blessing. And she has, apparently and rightfully, left all the creative decisions ultimately to the surviving Beatles.

Like cars on a train...when something affects one of The Beatles, it affects all of them. So, because of Yoko's enormous effect on John and her collateral effect on Paul, George and Ringo...and The Beatles collectively, Yoko Ono makes the list as The Beatles 35th Most Memorable Moment.

#34 - BANGLADESH

The verse at the beginning of the song that preceded the concert by only a couple of days really said it all. *"My friend came to me with sadness in his eyes. Told me that he wanted help before his country dies"*.

While they were doing post production on a film they did for Apple, Ravi Shankar told George Harrison about the plight of the Bengali people who were left homeless as a result of the Bangladesh Liberation War in 1971. Ravi hoped to do a benefit concert himself to raise $25,000 to help the people of his country. Harrison was moved strongly enough to not only help himself, but to ask everyone to help... becoming not only a performer at the concert, but its promoter. The concept was expanded from a concert featuring Shankar alone to one presenting an array of rock talent never before seen together on one stage.

George began contacting his friends. Leon Russell said "yes". Eric Clapton would appear, though his health was an issue. Billy Preston would be there.

Badfinger would come along. On the day before the concert, Bob Dylan agreed to perform. Mick Jagger was kept away only because of a lack of a visa. Ringo was there early on and, yes, a Beatles reunion was discussed. John agreed to be part of it, but, then, backed out when he discovered that Yoko was not to be included. And Paul stayed away because apparently he felt it was too soon after the break-up to have The Beatles perform on the same stage again, though, apparently, there was word that he would have shown up had Harrison agreed to sign off on the legal dissolution of the band.

But, even with only half The Beatles on stage, it was more than enough to carry the show. Two shows, in fact. Legendary. Spectacular. It would have been a significant event in rock history even if it wasn't happening to save the lives of people starving half way around the world.

'Bangladesh" is often said to be the rock's first charity concert. In fact, it wasn't. Elvis raised $65,000 at a benefit concert at Pearl Harbor in 1961. The Beatles themselves were part of a concert at the end of their first American tour...for which tickets cost $100 apiece...large money compared to the $5 you'd normally pay to see The Beatles back them...to benefit charities like United Cerebral Palsy. However, the "Bangladesh" single was pop music's first charity single.

And The Concert For Bangladesh was the first time rock came together as a community to help others. Probably, also, the first time a concert was held to help people in need half a world away. And the first time performers from such an idealistic time would do something this public to demonstrate the importance of living those ideals.

The concert itself raised more than $243,000...nearly ten times more than Ravi Shankar hoped for. The triple album it produced brought in $15 million more, but the release of the album was held up for two months because of haggling between record companies over giving permission for its artists to appear on the LP. This going on while people were dying of starvation. Harrison himself had to cut a check to help the relief efforts in the meantime.

Beyond that, the delay put George behind schedule in completing his follow-up to "All Things Must Pass" which slowed the momentum of his solo career, which he would never regain.

The US and UK governments held the money in escrow for years... not allowing it to be used. And, ultimately, apparently, little of the money found its way to those most in need. But, eventually, more money would be raised with the release of the concert on video. Then its re-release on DVD along with the re-issuing of the concert on CD.

No one would have blamed him if George decided thereafter to let the rest of the world take care of itself. Of course, he didn't. He formed the Material World Charitable Foundation. Later, contributed music... his own and that of the Traveling Wilburys to an effort...initiated by Olivia Harrison but sponsored by all four Beatle wives...to raise money and consciousness for the starving children of Romania. Harrison would also advise Bob Geldof when the former Boomtown Rat was putting together Live Aid...so even the mistakes that were made with 'Bangladesh' served a purpose.

The Beatles sang about changing the world and George Harrison did more than sing about it. He put his words into action. For all the controversy years earlier, The Beatles proved themselves not to be more popular than Jesus, as it turned out, they also spent a good deal of time and energy...as Jesus did...feeding the hungry.

Another example of one Beatles' sainted work canonizing the rest of the band. The Concert For Bangladesh. The Beatles 34th Most Memorable Moment.

#33 - LONDON PALLADIUM

Up until October 13th, 1963, The Beatles had been a not so quiet little secret kept by a growing number of British youth. Their records had become consistent #1's...However, hit 45's were the domain of teenagers. But, they had done enough TV and radio in their homeland... and built their recording career to the point where they had worked their way to "Sunday Night At The London Palladium"...a program that made its debut eight years earlier, on the first night of commercial TV in Great Britain and had become a viewing tradition in homes across England. The end of the weekend and you sat back and tuned in for an evening's worth of big names, top stars and "Beat The Clock". (Yeah, the classic American game show was part of 'Palladium', too.) Everybody who was anybody appeared on the show...Liberace, Chubby Checker, Sammy Davis, Jr., Hope and Keen. (I have no idea.)

For all the television The Beatles had done, this was the first time they were appearing on a show not aimed at teenagers, but at the entire family. It was the first time British adults were exposed to the frenzy The Beatles caused...on stage and in the audience. And, because of the stature of the 'Palladium' program, it was the first time the British press was exposed to the mania.

The group did four songs for their screaming audience (and screams could be heard from fans both inside and outside the Palladium)..."From Me To You"...their recent hit...both sides of their then current single, "She Loves You" and "I'll Get You" and, after John told the kids to 'shut up' (and he got applause for that from the adults in the seats), "Twist & Shout".

Even though they made only a paltry £250...about $750 in our money at the time, it was certainly a pinnacle for The Beatles. With this, they knew they had made it. And, by the end of their performance, everyone in Britain would know it, too. Their appearance was covered on the late evening network news that night. The next day, the front pages of newspapers all over Britain detailed the band's performance and the mania both inside the theatre and out. And, in fact, one of the headline writers called it "Beatlemania"...popularizing the term. A pop band literally making headline news. And, with that, The Beatles became a feel good sensation all over Britain, surprisingly, to me, anyway, only about three months before they conquered the US.

They did not set ratings records for their appearance on "Sunday Night At The Palladium". They pulled an audience of 15 Million viewers, impressive but far behind the 20 Million people who watched Cliff Richard's appearance three years before. But, that episode...or any other...couldn't have created the buzz across England that The Beatles did that night. In America today, considering the state of TV journalism, giving news time over to talk about a rock group being on a TV show would be commonplace, but not there and, certainly, not then.

Oddly enough, as popular as the show was, as was the case with American TV, virtually none of the broadcasts survive...only 5 out of 126 shows remain. Blessedly...another Beatles' miracle...the group's debut was one of them.

And that landmark visit in mid-October of '63 wasn't the group's only appearance on the show. They'd return once more...in mid-January of '64 which unintentionally served as something of a warm up for their Ed Sullivan show appearance. (And it's a shame that one doesn't survive. It would give us the one piece of video that existed of The Beatles doing "Money" live...part of that second show's set list.)

Still, the one that is still around captured a phenomenon. A country falling in love with four kids all at once. More than one out of 4 Brits were watching as Beatlemania was being created...figuratively and literally. It was an unforgettable night for Great Britain and a pivotal night for the band. And it set the stage for what would happen worldwide within about 100 days.

The Beatles' appearance on "Sunday Night At The London Palladium" was the band's 33rd most memorable moment.

#32 - FROM ME TO YOU

Why did some artists need to take four minutes to do a great record when The Beatles could do that in half the time? Well, we'll let that bit of rhetorical interrogation hang there. "From Me To You" is the first Beatles hit single to make our Top 50. And, more than a third of the way up, too.

Not all of them made it...not many of them, in fact. Like we said at the beginning of this thing, commercial success alone doesn't get you a ticket to the party. There has to be more to it than that...even for a record as good as this one is. In the case of "From Me To You", it got to #32 on our list because it was The Beatles second #1 single. Now, you may be thinking that that's some kind of back-handed honor... like being the second guy to invent the wheel. Not in the case of the music business. For many artists, following up a huge record is a tough... ultimately impossible thing to do. If you don't believe me, ask Debby Boone or Michael Damian or, even, Carl Perkins.

In comparison to getting your second #1 single, your first is almost easy. That's what was facing The Beatles coming off of "Please Please Me". They had gotten to the top, all right, but the pressure was on. Anything less than another major, major success could have labeled these guys as one hit wonders. A short shelf life on the British charts. Going back to the Cavern and, maybe, fourth or fifth billing on national tours, on the strength of their only hit. And forget anything happening for them in America. And I probably would have been doing The Paul Anka Show all these years. But enough scaring myself, they knew they needed another smash and the pop machine that would make Pepsi and Coke envious...Lennon and McCartney...went to work.

Inspiration came while The Beatles were touring with Helen Shapiro. The band was on the tour bus going from one town to another and John and Paul were just fooling around on their guitars. The melody began to come...bluesier than we would hear. John got the first line of lyric. (They would realize, after the fact, that the title came from the letters column in New Musical Express, a British pop newspaper of long standing.) And, by the time, they reached their destination, they knew their musical journey would just keep going. The Beatles had their second chart topper.

McCartney would later call the song "pivotal" to the group's success. He knew that the group had made it when he heard a mailman whistling the song one day. (And Paul also swears he heard a bird singing it.) And, he was right. The single was the first one from The Beatles to debut in the top ten...a sign that they had nothing left to prove. Their songs were not just instant adds with radio programmers, but instant hits with their fans. Ultimately, "From Me To You" proved to be The Beatles' biggest British chart single...spending 7 weeks at #1.

But it was significant for a couple of other reasons. The move to a minor chord in the bridge showed that John and Paul were already experimenting, trying to grow as songwriters. Not being satisfied...then or ever...with re-writing their hits over and over.

Also, here in America, where The Beatles failed famously until 1964, "From Me To You", at least, showed the slightest glimmer of success. It was The Beatles' first US chart record...making it to #118 in Billboard. Not a great number by any stretch, but it did show that some radio stations in some parts of America were playing The Beatles' music and some people were buying it. That had to help in some small way to begin to get the US familiar with The Beatles' sound.

Just look what else was happening with rock and roll at that time. People like Bobby Vinton and Chubby Checker were rock stars...C'mon. Quit laughing...And songs like "Sukiyaki" and "Hello Muddah, Hello Faddah" were hitting #1. Considering the state of the art...so to speak... and what happened to every other pre-1964 Beatles single in America, even hitting #118 could be called a success.

And the song itself is significant, too. While The Beatles' version of "From Me To You" didn't make the Top 100 in the Summer of '63, a version by Del Shannon did. Again, not a big hit...making it only to #73, but it did show that the group's music (Shannon's arrangement was identical to The Beatles') could, in fact, find an audience in America. And it was the first time there was any hint in America of John and Paul writing hits for other artists.

The people at Vee Jay probably regretted what was really a well-considered decision to hedge their bets and put two British number ones on one American single...pairing "From Me To You" with "Please Please Me"...knowing only The Beatles' lack of success to that point in the States and being able to flip the record over if the original 'A' side failed (again) to have much impact.

But, even as the undercard, "From Me To You" wound up being one of The Beatles' more successful 'B' sides...reaching #19 in Variety's chart...but it probably would have been a #1 if it had headed up a single of its own.

But, all told, it was the first song of theirs that someone else covered and charted with in the US. It was also the first record of theirs that charted in America and, by hitting #1 back home, it showed that the band were becoming consistent hit makers...a consistency that continues today. For all those reasons, "From Me To You" is The Beatles 32nd Most Memorable Moment.

#31 - HOLLYWOOD BOWL

There should be an entertainment industry adage..."If you're in show business long enough, at some point, you make it to Los Angeles". (Believe me, from experience, I know that's not necessarily a good thing.) But, in the case of The Beatles, long enough meant August 23rd, 1964. And that's one of the reasons why The Beatles' concerts at the Hollywood Bowl made our list...the location.

Los Angeles...Hollywood. The show business capital of the world... Paul McCartney would call it something like that decades later in the Anthology.

For The Beatles, their career had become a progression. They conquered Hamburg. Then, they came home and conquered Liverpool. Then all of England. Then America.

But it is one thing to move from playing in front of a couple of dozen drunks or even thousands of screaming kids to having to prove yourself in front of your peer group. And that's what Hollywood had to have been to The Beatles. Like heaven to the saints, if you're anybody in the entertainment industry, you wind up in Hollywood. Even by the fifth night of their American summer tour of '64, the guys had to have grown weary of this routine of playing the same dozen songs every night that the audience and the band couldn't hear, jumping in and out of armored cars, being imprisoned in hotels...even the best ones. But tonight would be different. The biggest names in every area of the business...TV and film as well as music...would be watching you...some of them with a jaundiced eye. If they were going to show the stars still more famous than them that they belonged...this was the night. You talk about pressure.

Besides that, the band had to know that they were going to be recorded. Capitol Records rolled out its mobile recording unit to North Highland near Fairfax. Voyle Gilmore...who produced Sinatra, Judy Garland and the Kingston Trio would be supervising the recording. This was going to be a document...a permanent record...literally. They couldn't slag this one off.

And, besides that, there was the venue itself. There's something magical about anything with the word 'Hollywood' in it. (Maybe not always...There are actually 'Hollywood Bowls' in Lincoln, Nebraska, Portland, Oregon and Batesville, Arkansas.)

Maybe I should say that there's something magical about something with the word 'Hollywood' in it and you're in Southern California and you're talking about show business. And 'the Bowl' certainly helped to build that legend. Its classic structure was designed by Frank Lloyd Wright's son in 1927 but it opened five years earlier and has been the home of the LA Philharmonic ever since. The greatest names in classical music played there. Franklin Roosevelt spoke there. Baryshnikov danced there. So did Fred Astaire. Billie Holiday, Al Jolson and Ella Fitzgerald would play there...and, now, The Beatles would too. The first rock act to perform at the Bowl. The Beatles would be playing on hallowed ground.

OK, that sets things up as to why the concert...going in...was so important. But, as for the concert itself, there's one more reason why 'Hollywood Bowl' made our list. Again, it's location, location, location. Where in Hollywood that the Bowl is located. Nestled comfortably in the hills above Hollywood, actually. Very accessible hills. Accessible to those not lucky enough to get a ticket to the show. Thousands and thousands and thousands of people not lucky enough. The man who promoted the concert, the great game show host, Bob Eubanks, said that, to be sure, the hills were alive that night in 1964. Beyond the nearly 19,000 people who bought tickets to the concert, he estimated that more than four times that many more kids climbed the hills for the chance to get as close to that Beatles' concert as they were going to get. (And Lennon pretty much proved it when during the concert he gave a "Welcome to you in the trees.")

Eubanks figured that there were more than 100,000 people there that night. Easily the biggest audience The Beatles would ever play in front of. Probably the biggest American rock concert until Woodstock and, maybe, the biggest single crowd to ever gather anywhere in the US to see one band perform. And Eubanks had no reason to inflate those figures. Remember, he made nothing on the concert beyond the 18,700 tickets he sold. He'd be bragging about all the money he lost.

The show itself? Exciting. Captivating. An absolute time stamp event. you might be able to say that about any Beatles concert, but, for the reasons we've stated, this one was very different.

As for what would be left for the world to listen to, unfortunately, those recording decks in Capitol's mobile unit couldn't hear the concert any better than The Beatles or their fans could. The tape of the show was only a three track recording and the whole of it was saturated by the tsunami of sound waves coming from the non-stop screams from those "healthy young lungs", as George Martin would later describe them.

After they listened to the results, The Beatles wouldn't think of issuing the tapes. They weren't satisfied with their performances and the fans already had versions of these songs on Beatle singles and albums. Years later, though, at the request of the President of Capitol Records, Bhaskar Menon, Sir George Martin revisited the tapes. No, the performances hadn't improved, but he was impressed by the electricity he heard. Martin knew this was part of The Beatles career... what they could do live...that had never been chronicled. (Remember, he wanted The Beatles first LP to be one of their sets at the Cavern.) The 'Hollywood Bowl' tapes, flawed as they were, were the only chance to do that. So, he agreed to see what he could do.

He and Beatles engineer, Geoff Emerick, labored over the tapes and pieced together a concert containing the highlights of shows from both 1964 and '65. They did a marvelous job...providing as much genius and wizardry as they had when The Beatles were with them in the studio.

By 1977, The Beatles all gave their consent. 'Hollywood Bowl' came out...the first time we'd heard new music from the band since 1970. The record became a #1 album for the group...seven years after they split. No other band had so great a success so long after they'd broken up.

The performances were, in fact, not letter perfect. Not every note was right. Not every piece of harmony came right on cue. But it was like the spirit of the law being more important than the letter of it. If you wanted perfect performances, listen to the studio work. 'Hollywood Bowl' was spectacular because of the non-stop energy the concert... and the album generated...from the stage to the stands and back again. It is frankly one of the best live albums of all time simply because of audio voltage it generates. If you can hear adrenaline, you hear it on "The Beatles At The Hollywood Bowl". The album was as much a part of The Beatles' story as 'Sgt. Pepper' or "Abbey Road". And it, eventually, became The Beatles' LP most demanded to be issued on CD by their fans.

So, ultimately, for showing us better than anything else how Beatlemania sounded in 1964...and how strong it still was more than a decade later, The Beatles' concerts at the Hollywood Bowl are Most Memorable Moment #31.

#30 - 'THE WHITE ALBUM'

The 'White Album' is an amazing work...for a lot of reasons. For one, I can't think of another album...from The Beatles or anyone else that covered as much musical ground. You heard dance hall music on it, folk, metal, big band, experimental, country and western, surf, lush ballads, political commentary, love songs, nonsense lyrics, story songs and straight ahead pop. As George Martin listened to the material before the band formally recorded it, he urged them to pare the songs down to the best 14 or so and release just a single album. As brilliant as he was, this time, Sir George was wrong. The Beatles needed that bigger canvas to present such a wide variety of music...to show the depth and breadth of their skills. Even the lesser songs...even the knock-off, screw around stuff like "Wild Honey Pie" fit in the context of so grand a program.

And the album is sequenced together so wonderfully. The more pop stuff...generally speaking...on disc one. The heavier stuff on disc two. No songwriter had more than two songs in a row. The animal songs..."Blackbird", "Piggies" and "Rocky Raccoon" were placed next to one another as a joke...as were the last three songs on side 2...to form a question and answer. "Why Don't We Do It In The Road?" "I Will, Julia".

And, it's odd that an album formally called "The Beatles" would feature four individual pictures of the band as the only photographs on its immaculately white outer sleeve. But those told the story, more than the name of the LP, as to where the band was at and where they were headed. Even after their greatest success..."Sgt. Pepper"...cracks in the foundation could be seen by those closest to the band. This was the first album they were recording after Brian Epstein's death and Paul continued to try to fill his role. But again, he appeared to be trying to be the most equal of the four equal members of the band. During the sessions for the album, McCartney's desire for perfectionism led him to record his own drumming over Ringo's, causing The Beatles' drummer to leave the band. Yoko was now a presence...John was both distracted by her and influenced by her...with tracks like "Revolution #9" and "What's The New Mary Jane" being evidence. Apple was becoming a source of greater and greater stress. And the band was facing a deadline in order for the album to be in the stores in time for the holidays. So, during a number of the sessions, different Beatles would be working in different studios on different songs at the same time. (Maybe that's why the band was able to cut more than twice as many songs in less time than it took for them to finish 'Sgt. Pepper'.)

And all of that began to take its toll. Geoff Emerick had enough of the ego and the in-fighting and he quit. George Martin went on a month's vacation in the middle of the sessions. A sign that the atmosphere had become so thick that even the group's mentor could no longer stand being around it. And The Beatles, more or less, wound up producing themselves.

It is amazing that the album was as cohesive as it turned out to be. The 'White Album' is sometimes called 'the first Beatles solo album' but, really, that does more to get a laugh than to get to the truth. As you listen to the album, you still hear Ringo's drumming, Paul's bass, George's guitar. There's a lesser use of harmonies on this than probably on any other Beatles' album, but, they're there, too. And, oddly enough, as probably only The Beatles could do, the scope of the album...the differences in style, tone and message from song to song...is probably what kept it together for an hour and a half.

Classic songs came from these sessions..."While My Guitar Gently Weeps", "Happiness Is A Warm Gun", "Obladi Oblada", "Back In The USSR". All brilliant...and those are just the starters. The sad thing, of course, was that it was during these sessions that the seeds of discontent among the band were sewn. And, within less than a year, the four of them would play together for the last time.

Sad because the album showed just how wide the scope of The Beatles talents had become and how much great music they could still make even when they were at each other's throats. And, regardless of that, how many more musical worlds they wanted to conquer together. (And it is probably the height of Beatle irony that the group would record their greatest anthem of unity, "Hey Jude" in the midst of all this infighting.)

As maybe their most ambitious work, The Beatles 'White Album' checks in as Most Memorable Moment #30.

#29 - LOVE ME DO

The inclusion of "Love Me Do" on our list was imperative. It moved The Beatles from being a local band...albeit a phenomenally popular one...to being a band that was playing to all of England. The record was not a huge success...making it only to #17...not bad at all for a group's first single (and there were strong rumors that the only reason why the disc charted that high was because Brian Epstein bought so many copies himself). And that was its best chart number across England. However, back home, in their local rock paper, "Mersey Beat", the single shot straight to #1. (Again, Brian's work might have helped here.)

That foreshadowed what would happen in weeks. The people in the North of England were already familiar with The Beatles, got their act, felt their vibe, whatever. So, "Love Me Do" was an immediate 'must have'. For the rest of the country, it was their introduction to The Beatles...getting them ready for everything that was to come.

Maybe a better gauge of how strong the record really was, is how it rose quickly to the top of the American charts when it was released over here. (The group's 6th #1 stateside.) Or how it climbed all the way into the British top 5 when it was re-released there in 1976. All The Beatles singles were re-issued in the UK back then...and none of them did as well as "Love Me Do". And it would be the highest charting Beatles single at home for a span of more than 25 years...from "Let It Be" to "Free As A Bird".

But, maybe one of the most important aspects of "Love Me Do" was that John and Paul wrote the song and they were insistent about it being their first single...even though George Martin had them work up and record their version of "How Do You Do It". Obviously, that song was strong, too. The version done by Gerry and the Pacemakers was a British #1 and an American top 5 and The Beatles' take on the song was, arguably, better.

But The Beatles wanted to be known more than as just singers or musicians. They wanted their reputation to be built on their skill as songwriters...as it was with many of their heroes...Chuck Berry, Carl Perkins and Little Richard. Though they were basically a cover band live, they had decided early on that their style, their growth, their success as recording artists would be determined by the songs they wrote...not the ones their managers or their record companies found for them (a la Elvis Presley, Rick Nelson, Frankie Avalon and we go down from there).

Of course, after several hundred remarkable songs written together and apart among all four of them in the decades that followed, who could argue with that choice? (And, indeed, the Achilles heel for virtually every huge star in pop music is their dependence on other people...songwriters...to maintain their success. The great songs stop coming...and they invariably do...so do the hits. The Beatles, to this day, would never have had that problem.)

But "Love Me Do" was really the genesis of the rock and roll band as self-contained musical unit..."We play the songs, we sing the songs"... and, with apologies to Barry Manilow and Bruce Johnston..."we write the songs". (Oddly enough, The Beatles' biggest influence on how they would operate as a band...four do-it-yourselfers...came not from Elvis or any of the other people we heard them mention so often, but from Bill Haley and his Comets. It was a formal band. They recorded together, played live together. They wrote many of the songs they sang. Bill sang lead...virtually always...and it was the Comets who'd sing in back of him. Yes, the template for The Beatles was not the king, but that round faced guy with the spit curl...and those six guys in the shiny red sport coats and bow ties along with him.

But The Beatles served as the template for everyone else. By the mid 60's, almost everybody was writing their own material. In fact, by the end of the decade, composers who'd made their money writing songs for others...like Carole King and Boyce and Hart...were recording their own material and having hits...maybe because there was nobody who wasn't writing their own songs to record them.

I can't think of a band today that doesn't write its own material and, if they do go outside to record something they didn't compose, it's a rock standard...often written by The Beatles.

So, for being the first success they recorded, the first success they wrote; and for basically laying the first paving stone for re-inventing the singer-songwriter...connecting Chuck Berry to James Taylor, oddly enough and for re-crafting the rock group as a rock band...a creative one stop shop that could control its own destiny; and by proving how well that could work and, most importantly, for opening the door for the decades of achievement that would come after, "Love Me Do" is The Beatles 29th Most Memorable Moment.

#28 - THE DEATH OF GEORGE HARRISON

I've got to tell you, I am still surprised by the enormous outpouring of emotion on the part of the whole world that came with the announcement of George's death.

He had been the most private Beatle. The one who ran the farthest from the group's legacy. In fact, the one who would denigrate that legacy longer and more frequently and to a greater degree than any other member of the band. And the one who, more than any other, never got his due when the band was together. A situation that, to a degree, carried on after the band parted. His solo albums were uniformly terrific and yet, with the exception of "All Things Must Pass", lesser works from other members of The Beatles were more highly acclaimed, sold better, produced more hits. He hadn't done a new album in nearly 15 years. And when his greatest opportunity to step back into the spotlight came…The Beatles' Anthology…he refused to meet with the press…giving interviews only by fax and headed out to hide in Hawaii as the TV mini-series debuted.

Still, when he passed, the world mourned as if he were in the public eye constantly.

It wasn't because his death came unexpectedly…as John Lennon's did…we knew he was sick. Knew it was cancer. Knew the surgeries to remove it were ultimately unsuccessful. And it wasn't because his impending death was all over the media. No one even knew where George was when he died. But the demonstration of grief when George left us was almost as great as when John died…more than 20 years earlier. A death that, really, took any chance of a Beatles reunion with it.

I think one of the reasons was that George died of throat cancer… Something that usually kills older people. For the first time, an icon of baby boomers left us through disease…not through self-indulgence, an act of mechanical fate or a madman's violent act. George's death reminded us about our own mortality. And that that mortality was beginning to approach all of us.

More than that, though, I think the reaction that came with the passing of George Harrison...and the response...the sales...of the DVD and CD of the "Concert For George" demonstrate just how much the world loved...loves...him and his music. Yes, it was a gathering of many of rock's greatest names...maybe the last great gathering of that generation of rock stars...including the first live appearance of Paul and Ringo together since The Beatles played Candlestick Park. That may have been part of it...but a small part. There were many packages like that and none sold like "The Concert for George" (Platinum ten times over). The buying of the video or the audio of the concerts, ultimately, was the way millions upon millions of people chose to say, "I love you, George...and I won't forget you". That, apparently, was the only way we could do it. For understandable reasons, George wouldn't give us the opportunity to do that while he was still alive

I don't think I ever discounted George Harrison's ability as a singer, songwriter, musician and humanitarian. I just discounted how many other people felt about him the same way I did.

In most cases where a pop musician dies (and death is the best of all promotional tools in rock and roll...if you don't believe me ask Buddy Holly, Jim Croce or Otis Redding), there is usually a quick and large spike in the sales of their music. Certainly there was for John. "(Just Like) Starting Over" was already falling from the top ten before Lennon's death, Within two weeks after it, though, it made a quick U-turn and headed up to #1.) But that spike is just as quick to stop. In John's case, it lasted through "Milk & Honey"...four years after he was killed. That was his last top ten album in the US, even though there were more entertaining, essential packages that would come after.

With George, there was "Brainwashed" (American top ten), followed by "The Concert For George" DVD (American Top 5). Then came "Let It Roll" (British top 4). Then came "George Harrison: Living In The Material World" DVD (American #1) and its companion CD, "Early Takes Volume 1" (American Top Ten). That's five major successes in less than ten years. But, if all of this was just the after effect of Harrison's passing, it wouldn't have gone on for a decade. It was merely a sign of how much the world loved George Harrison and his music. (He had said, while The Beatles were working on "Real Love", "I hope somebody takes all my crap demos when I'm dead (and) make(s) them hit records". Well, they weren't all demos...and none of them were crap.

But George has had a run of solo success that he never had when he was alive. And it probably worked out as he wished. He made the music and did nothing more. Didn't have to deal with record companies, the press and fans...all of whom Harrison probably found too crazy too often. And it worked out for us, too. We wind up getting more George Harrison music.

Just a guess here but, had Harrison lived we probably would never had gotten any of this. George would probably have kept making music for his entertainment, not ours...too much bother in too many ways to become Beatle George...or, even ex-Beatle George again. That is probably the only solace about Harrison leaving us and it's certainly not a reason for his passing making our list.

But this is the major reason why it did...and why it ranked so high. I don't know if you noticed, but, once George left us, there were no cries for Paul and Ringo to go back in the studio together. record an album and call it "The Beatles". Pete Townsend and Roger Daltrey did that with half the Who. No one called Paul and Ringo's appearance at the Concert for George a 'Beatles' reunion'. No, with George's death, any talk of The Beatles continuing as a band, making new music stopped. As of 11/29/01, The Beatles were no more.

And it became one more ironic twist in this marvelous story of The Beatles. That this most reticent Beatle...the one who couldn't get far enough away from The Beatles...would be the one to take the band with him when he died.

George Harrison's death...The Beatles 28th Most Memorable Moment.

#27 - CANDLESTICK PARK

It's amazing how peoples' patterns of behavior repeat themselves throughout life...even groups of people...like The Beatles. A few years later, when they were working on "Abbey Road", no one in the group's inner circle said that it would be the last time the four of them would work together in the studio, yet, pretty much everyone knew it. It was the same in 1966. By that time, the screaming girls, the James Bond-like escapes, the traveling all over the world to play the same 25 minutes worth of music their audience could hear anyway had long, long since stopped being enjoyable. And, by that time, it stopped being tolerable. With this last tour, they feared for their lives in the Philippines...actually being assaulted while trying to leave and, after John's remark about The Beatles and Jesus, they faced death threats from American nuts who wanted to defend the teachings of Christ by killing people. So, continuing to tour had become more than monotonous and stultifying, it had become dangerous. Again, no one said it, but everyone knew. This was the end of the road for The Beatles...literally. A final dozen songs. The last time they'd have to play "Rock and Roll Music" or "I Feel Fine" on stage...or anywhere else. Press officer, Tony Barrow, dutifully recorded the first 11 1/2 of them on a cassette recorder, as per Paul's request... McCartney probably sensing that this was it for The Beatles live. The tape ran out before the band finished "Long Tall Sally" and, apparently, the first few chords of "In My Life" before they gave a collective "What the F" and ran off stage for the last time.

In that final year of touring, particularly, they had become a schizophrenic rock act anyway. Doing one kind of music in the studio. Doing something entirely different...and not at all where they were at that point creatively...on the road. None of the songs they'd just recorded for "Revolver", the album that they, ideally, were touring to support were included on the set list...though some of them, like "Taxman" and "She Said She Said" certainly could have been. Much of the album featured too many outside musicians...strings and horns...or used things like tape loops or backwards guitars...to be re-created...in those days...on stage.

For years, The Beatles knew that their greatest creative outlet was the live concert. People who saw them at their zenith in that realm said they were amazing, unparalleled. They tore up Hamburg. Owned the Cavern. But that live dominance began to wither as they started having hits and were reduced to playing only 20 minute sets as they were part of multi-band tours in England...even as headliners. As that was going on, they were already starting to grow as artists in the studio. As the months and years went by, they would become more comfortable at Abbey Road and less so on the road. By the time they got to America, their act had been reduced to 'copy and paste' night after night. Life on stage had become rotten and, while on tour, life off stage was worse. And the band's attitude towards playing live affected their performance. By the tours in '66, their act had gone from sloppy but energetic to unprofessional and apathetic. (Did I hear somewhere that, when they were on stage in America, Lennon would routinely swear at the kids that loved him and the rest of the band knowing they couldn't hear him?) They just didn't care anymore. Brian Epstein finally understood and agreed to pull the band off the road.

It can't be coincidence that The Beatles' most innovative recorded work, "Sgt. Pepper" came in the year after the group was freed from touring and had become totally a studio entity. Had they stayed on the road, their time, their energy...physical and creative would have been sapped...flying all over everywhere, dealing with and trying to avoid their fans, and attempting to satisfy everyone on the planet who wanted just a minute with The Beatles.

Continuing to tour would cripple their development as more than singers, musicians or songwriters, but as conceptualizers of music. Their becoming men who were learning just what could be done to make music in a recording studio had already begun but really flourished fully when they left the road. Their choice was to continue to make music for thousands of people who couldn't hear it or to make it for millions of people who could. The choice was no choice at all.

The Beatles' last concert at Candlestick Park wasn't really the end of anything, as much as it was a beginning. And for that, it is The Beatles 27th Most Memorable Moment.

#26 - BRIAN EPSTEIN

Though he died while Sgt. Pepper was still the #1 album throughout pretty much of the whole world, Brian Epstein's effect on The Beatles can still be seen today. Much of the beloved image The Beatles still have now can be traced back to Brian cleaning up their act, putting them in suits, getting them to stop eating, stop smoking, stop swearing on stage. The fact that, in spite of their hair, The Beatles were well groomed, well dressed and polite did a great deal to undercut how threatening they first appeared to America's parents. Those first impressions insulated the band from the missteps they made while they were together and prevented any permanent damage from the individual bouts with insanity that each of them had after they broke up.

But, before that, it was Brian who when he first saw the band recognized in them something the world would later discover. The energy, the affability and, oh Lord, the talent to make music. He worked tirelessly to promote the group locally...getting friends to call record stores across the north of England to ask if they had the new release from the band. Labored to get them their Decca audition. When The Beatles failed with that, he took the tapes around London to see if anybody else would be interested in the band. Through his persistence, he met somebody who could put him together with George Martin, who gave them their audition and, ultimately, their contract with EMI.

It was Brian's skills as a negotiator that got The Beatles their top of the show billing on Ed Sullivan, long before they had anything close to resembling a hit in America. He set up the deals for "A Hard Day's Night" and "Help!" and all the merchandising that made The Beatles more omnipresent than Mickey Mouse or Bugs Bunny in 1964 America. He made good on every contract for every date The Beatles signed at small clubs and dink venues in England...even though he could have cancelled and re-booked the band for more money elsewhere. And he did it because it was the right thing to do.

He kept the press from devouring the band during the worst of the 'bigger than Jesus' crisis and probably saved their lives by paying off someone in the Philippines after the group's accidental snub of Imelda Marcos. And finally, agreed to let the band stop touring.

All because he loved them. Yes, he was gay, but I don't mean 'loved them' in that way. And it wouldn't have mattered if he did.

There was a story about his being present at a Beatles concert after the group hit. Things were pretty well under control, so Brian indulged himself. He went to the back of the house and screamed and yelled like all the other fans there. He understood probably on a conscious basis that the subtext to everything The Beatles did was excitement, exuberance, unbridled joy. You can hear that in their music...together and apart...even today.

Yes, he cost them money...probably a lot of money through the merchandising and record deals he made. But, looking back, did The Beatles ever need to have someone throw them a benefit? Part of the reason they continued to make the money they did decades after his death was because of the groundwork he first laid.

It can't be just happenstance that the personal problems within the band and the financial mess that Apple became both started within a year after Brian's death and the end of The Beatles itself came less than three years later. You don't need any more proof of Brian Epstein's importance to The Beatles than that.

His work made them so popular that he no longer needed to pursue people in the press to promote the band. They were pursuing him to get stories. And with the band no longer touring, much of his initial role with The Beatles had disappeared. There was talk that The Beatles might replace him when their contract lapsed in 1968. Ringo would later deny that. And it's hard to think that after all he did for The Beatles, they would turn their backs on him. He had taught them too well about doing what's right.

How important was Brian Epstein to The Beatles? Well, my feeling has, for a long time, been that, had he lived, they would never have broken up. They may have started doing solo work. The band may have worked like Crosby, Stills, Nash and Young. Do their own solo albums then, every few years, come together as The Beatles. It would have been the best of both worlds and it was an option apparently never discussed by The Beatles as they went their own ways and after.

But it might never have come down to that, anyway. Had Brian lived, Paul would never have felt the need to assert himself to the point of angering the other members of the band. Out of respect, The Beatles would have let Epstein mediate their personal differences...which would never have gotten to the point they did if Brian were still there.

What The Beatles...in the big picture...did with Brian Epstein alive can best be measured by what they did without him. Like anyone who's lost someone they really loved, the space they leave is greater than the one they filled. As John would say years later, "You don't know what you got until you lose it". The Beatles lost more than a manager when Brian took that overdose of pills and drink. They lost their patron saint.

Brian Epstein's discovering The Beatles and his tireless work to bring them success is The Beatles 26th Most Memorable Moment.

#25 - HAMBURG

So much that was essential to what The Beatles would become would happen to them while they were in Germany...or because they had to go there in the first place. The first thing was that the contract that sent the Silver Beatles (soon after arriving they changed it to just, The Beatles) John, Paul, George and Stuart Sutcliffe to Germany called for them to have a permanent drummer. That was what brought Pete Best into the group.

In fact, Hamburg would bring the group both of its best known drummers. Ringo would see the band perform...unimpressively in his mind...in the fall of 1960 while he was there playing with Rory Storm and the Hurricanes. At that time Ringo was much further ahead in terms of his career than the other future Beatles. In fact, they would actually play with him there...record with him, in fact, backing up Lu Walters, the Hurricanes' bass player, as he recorded a demo of Gershwin's "Summertime". Best was not at the session. Reportedly, he was out buying drumsticks, so it was John, Paul, George and Ringo playing in back of Lu...accidental epochal moment captured on a handful of acetates. (Six of them, with only one known to survive.) The irony is that The Beatles wanted to record some songs after Lu was finished but Allan Williams, the group's manager at that point, who paid for the session for Walters wouldn't spend any money on recording The Beatles because he didn't want the group to be late for that night's gig.

The Beatles themselves would sign their own first recording and publishing contract...with Bert Kaempfert and have their first experience in a real recording studio backing British singer Tony Sheridan and recording their first songs on their own ("Ain't She Sweet" and "Cry For A Shadow"). Hamburg was where Stuart Sutcliffe realized that he was an artist, not a musician and where he found the love of his life, Astrid Kirchherr and where he would choose to call home, leave The Beatles behind and sadly, die suddenly in April of 1962 at age 21.

But the most important purpose Hamburg played in The Beatles' story was to be the group's live laboratory. It was a place to give them the chance to experiment as live performers in the same way that Abbey Road would let them experiment as studio artists.

That contract they signed with Bruno Koschmider called for them to perform everyday...I mean, seven days a week. No days off. Playing nearly 35 hours every week. And, if you're working a 40 hour a week job and think they were getting off easy, try holding a guitar, playing it and singing for five hours a night every night for a week and see how you feel.

The Beatles would prove the adage that practice, in fact, does make perfect. The 15 week stay in Germany meant more than 500 hours on stage. You spend 500 hours doing anything...studying biology, playing rock and roll or robbing banks...and you're going to get good at it. The Beatles, of course, got more than good. Also, that much time on stage meant they had to have a broad repertoire and they did. They offered well over 100 songs...a growing number of them being Lennon-McCartney originals.

When they moved from the first venue they were booked into, the Indra Club, to the busier Kaiserkeller, where they found they'd be playing on a much larger stage than they'd ever done before. That intimidated them. At first, they pretty much seemed like five mannequins on stage until Allan Williams, shouted to them to 'Mach Shau'...German for "make a show". At that point, all The Beatles...except Pete Best, of course, began moving around the stage, writhing and contorting themselves. Their act began to work with their German audiences, who'd buy them beer and give them pills...uppers...that would keep them awake...and energized... through their long nights on stage. So, Hamburg also introduced The Beatles to the drug culture.

They would not only play for the audience. They would play with them. Yelling at them. Swearing at them. Lennon would come on stage with a toilet seat around his neck, call the people in the club 'Nazis'. The band would goose step on stage and wave swastikas...the Nazi flag. The Beatles' ability to rouse an audience into a frenzy...eventually turning into the lung straining screams of thousands of teenage girls...began right there. Like I said, with that much time on stage, they could experiment... In fact, they had to. They had to try new things, push themselves just to fill the hours. They had the time to find out what worked for them, what worked for their audience. They kept what worked, lost what didn't. And they acquired that magical gift you don't learn from guitar teachers...presence. And I don't know if you can learn charisma, but The Beatles found that there, too.

They would be thrown out of Germany in 1960...Harrison because he was underage, McCartney and Best for setting a fire in the room in which The Beatles stayed.

They were back, though, in March of 1961...for another 500+ hours on stage.

By the time they came back from that second trip, the group had polished their act to a high gloss. They were now ready to take Liverpool by storm...which they did. Within weeks of their return, Brian Epstein would see them perform and became sold on their potential and the rest would eventually become history. They would return to Hamburg twice more...2 trips for two weeks each in the fall and winter of 1962. By this time, they had begun recording for EMI, had appeared on the BBC and, like it would be, years later, for touring and, even, eventually, for working together, The Beatles had outgrown Hamburg.

Luckily, King Size Taylor and The Beatles had enough to drink one night that the group signed away the rights to three hours of their performances...while they were already under contract to EMI, by the way. The tapes gathered dust but ultimately became a fascinating, though sonically starved double album which gave us, probably, the last listen to The Beatles as a bar band. As tough as a listen is to those discs...from an audio standpoint only...you hear a rawness in The Beatles music that had to be a major factor in the group connecting with their audience. A listen to virtually anything from those sets played next to a track from their Decca audition gives you undeniable proof of the amazing growth the band experienced in just 12 months and shows you why they would begin taking England by storm in less than 90 days.

But for being part of their story at so many points, The Beatles days in Hamburg were the group's 25th most memorable moment.

#24 - THE BEATLES' 1964 CHART ATTACK

There is the saying that figures can lie, but these figures don't. Where do we start?

Well, "Can't Buy Me Love" was the #1 record in America that most famous week in April of 1964 when The Beatles actually had all five of the top five singles in America. And that was going to be it for us. Obviously, seeing that nobody has ever had more than two singles in the top five, before or since, that would probably be enough to get it a place on our top 50. But what The Beatles did on the charts that year was so, so much more than, that we couldn't stop there. They also had the top 5 in Cashbox, too...with a different #1, "Twist & Shout".

Actually, the week after they had the top 5, they did something that was, arguably even more impressive. They had fourteen different singles on Billboard's Hot 100...and a 15th on its 'Bubbling Under' chart. One out of every seven records on the singles chart came from The Beatles.

But, hang on. In Billboard, The Beatles actually succeeded themselves in #1 twice. "I Want To Hold Your Hand" replaced by "She Loves You" replaced by "Can't Buy Me Love". That was a record that went unequaled until Usher had three #1's in a row in 2004. But, we found out that The Beatles, in fact, had four #1's in a row in Cashbox..."Twist & Shout" hitting the top in between "She Loves You" and "Can't Buy Me Love" and we thought that was the record.

But we, just prior to our writing the arc of programs for The Beatles Show that this whole book is based on, got our hands on copies of another national record chart...from the Teletheatre Research Institute...This survey was syndicated in newspapers back then and was, really, the only national music chart that the record buying public could get its hands on every week. In that chart, "Can't Buy Me Love" was actually succeeded at #1 by "Do You Want To Know A Secret" and, on the Teletheatre survey, that gave The Beatles 5 consecutive #1's...and that is a record...meaning an accomplishment, not a piece of vinyl, that nobody could possibly ever equal. And, beyond that, it gave the group five #1 singles in their first four months on the American charts.

But that's not it either. From the last day "I Want To Hold Your Hand" stayed at #1 in Billboard...March 14th, 1964 to the first day "Eight Days A Week landed there...March 13th, 1965...364 days...The Beatles would have ten different #1 singles (in one major chart or another...or all of them, really.)

To give you some perspective, the wonderfully talented and popular Whitney Houston was 7th all time in terms of having #1 singles. In the course of a 20 + year career, she's had 11 of them. The Beatles, in a year, came up one short of what she did in her entire professional life.

Anybody come close? Elvis would be a logical answer, but the king could only do half as well as The Beatles...hitting the top five times in 1956. You want any real competition, you have to go back to the 1930's to find bandleader Paul Whiteman who had 7 number ones in that year and, in 1964, The Beatles trumped that by almost half again.

And, wait, there's more, still. In addition to all those #1's, The Beatles had two records reach #2..."PS I Love You", blocked from #1 by "Love Me Do" and "She's A Woman"...which would eventually get to #2, blocked from #1 by "I Feel Fine". One reached #3..."Please Please Me", blocked from #1 by both "I Want To Hold Your Hand" and "She Loves You" in Billboard, Cashbox and Record World...though it did get to number #1 for a pair of weeks on American Bandstand's Top Ten. And "I Saw Her Standing There" would also reach the top ten and, on Bandstand, so would "And I Love Her". That's more than a dozen top ten singles in one year...almost as many as people like Connie Francis, the Temptations, the Everly Brothers and the Four Seasons would have through the length of their entire careers.

That's still not all. Songs like "Ain't She Sweet", "Matchbox" and "I'll Cry Instead" would just miss making the top ten. In all, The Beatles would have six more singles reach the top 20. Three more hit the top 30. One more hit the top 40. All told, that year alone, The Beatles had 31 different records reach our national singles charts....racking up a total of 257 weeks on the charts that year...Meaning The Beatles averaged nearly five records on the singles chart each week for an entire year. (Really more than that because they didn't hit the charts until three weeks into 1964.)

If you weren't around in 1964, then, your idea of how big The Beatles were that year might be confined to your DVD's of Ed Sullivan or "A Hard Day's Night". But they were everywhere. Forget any superstars today. Forget the biggest movies or the highest rated TV shows. Nobody was ever bigger than The Beatles were in 1964...and the fact that glow has hardly dimmed in 50 years is exhibit A class evidence.

But, if you want the real story...with numbers to back it up, check the internet for sites that have old music charts. Look and see how dominant The Beatles were for the entire year. The proof...and the truth...is all there in black and white.

Then, you'll understand why people say there was never anything like The Beatles before they came along...or after, either.

For their remarkable, historic, unequaled accomplishments on the American records charts, The Beatles 1964 Chart Attack is the group's 24th Most Memorable Moment.

#23 - HEY JUDE

The Beatles were beginning to crumble internally, but "Hey Jude" might have been the public pinnacle of their career. It would be their biggest American single...nine weeks at #1 and, certainly, their most majestic. And it was a great example...possibly the best one...of how The Beatles subtly...probably unconsciously...delivered their message. Most likely, speaking from their own hearts and, in the course of that, touching the hearts of the entire world.

The song, of course, was written by Paul to John's first son, Julian, to comfort him through his parents' divorce. McCartney would broaden the lyrics so everyone could relate...really, turning it into a love song but it said so much more than that. If you study those simple words, what they're really saying jumps out at you. "Don't take it bad" reminded us not to get discouraged. "Take a sad song and make it better" was really telling us to take what we're given and make the most of it...rather than complain about us not having enough. And the last two lines of that first verse..."Remember to let her into your heart, then you can start to make it better" telling us...almost word for word that 'we can make it better'. And the song went on from there. It was the same message of hope The Beatles have delivered time and again, alone and together, from the start, but maybe never better than here.

The video of the song was epic, too. The Beatles appearing live again...not playing, really, but singing live. With a full orchestra in back of them and, then, during the long climax, the stage flooded with the group's fans. There were seemingly members of every different demographic group. Young people, Old people. Men and women. People of different races. And it seemed like everyone on earth was represented.

I am sure that The Beatles never intended for this to happen, but what you saw unmistakably as you watched the "Hey Jude" video was The Beatles bringing the whole world together.

At 7:11, was it a little self-indulgent? Well, perhaps, but, let me ask you...where would you fade it out? The majesty of the whole song justified its length. It was a magnificent vocal performance building from diminuendo to crescendo...quieter to louder...and back again...as the best classical music does. A wonderful dynamic range of emotion expressed in Paul's singing. And I'll tell you this until the time when the record was ready to drop off the charts, no radio station dumped the end of "Hey Jude". Yeah, asking stations to play a seven minute record was a lot. But, look at it this way, they could play another top 5 single and something from the, say, top 25 or what would become the #1 song of the year...and, by the way, it was from The Beatles. Who won that argument?

Even with Dylan's "Like A Rolling Stone" (6:13) and Richard Harris' "MacArthur Park" (7:20) months before, it was, as always, when The Beatles did something, it was sanctified. And the door was opened for longer and longer recordings...meaning you can give some of the blame for Elton's "Someone Saved My Life Tonight" (a dirge that went on for 6:45. Did that song ever end, by the way?) and Paul's "Silly Love Songs" (far too silly to last 5:53) to The Beatles.

The group proving that old slogan for Winston Super Kings..."It's not how long you make it. It's how you make it long". (And The Beatles themselves showed restraint by not issuing the full ten minute version of "Hey Jude" as they initially wanted to do.)

And, here's another way this release wound up being 'landmark'. The Beatles, probably more than anyone else in the music business, developed the whole idea of 'new release as an event'. Before this, you always had to have a record out. Elvis was gone from the charts for only about a month or so from 1956 through the mid 60's. How was one record different, more special than the other...(The whole idea of that was that, if you were gone from the radio for any length of time, your audience might forget about you.)

But The Beatles changed that...along with a moving van full of other things...too. Of course, it started with the Sullivan show appearances. Not much bigger an event that that. Then, they had two albums come out concurrently with their first film and their first US tour. Same thing a year later. (And please don't suggest that the band was just copying Presley. Did anybody rush out to buy "Big Boss Man" because it was in "Clambake"?) In '66, The Beatles didn't have a movie, but they did have the whole 'Hey, we're more popular than God' thing. (The old saying is 'any kind of publicity is good publicity...Maybe not in this case.) Then came 'Pepper' and "Our World"...and the debut of their new single to everyone of the planet. After that came a TV special to hype their next 45 and EP. But, with "Hey Jude", The Beatles actually did things the other way around. This was going to be a single meant to promote a record label. "Hey Jude" was the first 45 released on Apple. It wasn't imperative that it be a one of a kind record. I mean, these were The Beatles. It was going to be a huge hit, anyway. But, again, perhaps unintentionally, the group produced an especially remarkable record...and, for The Beatles, that was saying a lot, to give their new label...and all the other artists on it...an additional push. Leave it to The Beatles to turn a record industry axiom upside down and still have it work perfectly.

The Beatles majestic biggest single of all...and so much more than that..."Hey Jude" is The Beatles 23rd Most Memorable Moment.

#22 - A HARD DAY'S NIGHT

With each new release, even in those heady days of Beatlemania, it seemed, The Beatles still faced some new challenges. First, they had to find some way to follow "I Want To Hold Your Hand"...as was the case when they had to write a follow up to "Please Please Me" and they came up with "From Me To You". If everything went absolutely wrong and they put out a flop...even with all the hype, even with all the momentum, they'd be finished. Again, they met the challenge, this time with "Can't Buy Me Love".

Then they had to find some way to follow that and to introduce their first movie...pre-sell it, if you will. And they certainly did with "A Hard Day's Night". Just a great track that reinforced the idea...probably removed all doubt...that these guys weren't going to go away.

The album that featured music from "A Hard Day's Night" added even more to the reputation of Lennon and McCartney as songwriters. This was the first album from The Beatles that was written completely in house...all the songs coming from John and Paul. And great songs, too. Beyond the title tune, "I Should Have Known Better" was an enormous worldwide hit and "If I Fell" and "And I Love Her" were the first classic love songs that John and Paul wrote. And, surprisingly, most of them were written in about a week, total.

But the record itself wasn't the reason why "A Hard Day's Night" made our top 50. The film that carried its name was another example of The Beatles teaming up with someone almost as young and just as brilliant in another area. That someone, in this case, was Richard Lester. The Beatles had become Lester fans after they saw "The Running Jumping Standing Still Film" he had directed. To write the film Lester brought in Alun Owen who had been his partner for a short lived TV series. They watched the mania that surrounded the group in the Fall of 1963 and the film pretty much wrote itself. The Producer, Walter Shenson, gave them a budget...only $500,000...not much to make a movie, even then. Like a good writer, Owen wrote to budget and, like a good director, Lester shot to it. His idea was to create a "factionalized"... as he would call it...story of The Beatles...shoot it in black and white, like a documentary...again to compensate for budget limitations and, then add some surreal elements to make the songs fit in.

Well, that was the whole key. Lester brought in so many elements... few of which had been used often in any kind of cinema, much less in what had been the knock off kind of movies done to showcase rock stars. Film was sped up, slowed down. There were amazingly quick cuts. Far more camera movement that we were used to. And that surreal element. There was that memorable sequence when the group encountered a snobbish gentleman on the train. Suddenly, we saw the four of them outside the train running after it. Then they were back inside again.

There was the sequence done for "I Should Have Known Better". The band is in the baggage car playing poker, then, suddenly, they have their instruments and they're playing a song. All that made it clear this wasn't a documentary, but it wasn't like any movie we'd seen either. And though you could probably trace the music video back to Al Jolson and "The Jazz Singer" and before, the way Richard Lester used film to present music in "A Hard Day's Night" was certainly the beginning of the modern music video, and, with it, the faster pace and the use of more camera effects on all movies and TV shows and commercials. And The Beatles, though not being seen as the creators of all these innovations, were certainly seen as the reason for them. Yeah, The Beatles gave us MTV...and ADD, too.

And, beyond that, regardless of how much their fans read about them or heard them in interviews, once they saw them in "A Hard Day's Night", the images of the four Beatles were set in stone...covered in Kryptonite. John would be the tough guy, the leader. Paul would be the romantic. George would be the quiet Beatle and Ringo would the cuddly one. Those stereotypes...all positives, by the way...and there were probably elements of truth in all of them...would hang with The Beatles for the rest of their lives.

It also made them more than rock stars, it made them movie stars and, by doing a film so groundbreaking, it was probably the first real step in elevating them above Elvis Presley...if not in the level of success... though that would happen, too...then in the quality of the work.

So, for creating The Beatles images...on screen and off and for changing movie making in many of the same ways The Beatles changed music making and for the beginning of the dethroning of the king, "A Hard Day's Night" is The Beatles 22nd Most Memorable Moment.

#21 - RUBBER SOUL

If The Beatles went on "Beat The Clock", they'd have won every refrigerator in Goodson/Todman's prize warehouse.

It is one thing to be great. It is quite another to be great and do it in a hurry. But that's what The Beatles were looking at.

1965 was a little less frenzied than 1964 was...but not by much. They did 50 less live shows...and didn't have to venture all the way to Australia for any of them. Cut way back on their TV appearances. They were done with BBC radio. (At this point, why do it? They'd been promoting the shows they'd be going on more than themselves.)

They made another movie...but "Help!" took a month longer to shoot than "A Hard Day's Night".

And there has to be some question as to whether or not they had any chance to rest up from the last year's worth of Beatlemania.

Still, they owed EMI a new album and a new single for Christmas. They faced the same situation at the end of 1964 and wound up doing "Beatles For Sale"...heavy on covers and weak on new material... relatively speaking. The group was simply tapped...and the bedraggled looks on their faces on the cover shows it.

Was it going to be the same way in 1965? Well, it could have been worse. The group began their sessions for "Beatles For Sale" in August of 1964, finishing them in mid-October for an early December release of the album. This year, The Beatles would begin recording on October 12 with the album needing to be wrapped up by...November 11th...In the words of Chuck Berry, "thirty days".

Oh, and, one more thing...Even though the band had had six weeks off from the end of their second American tour and the beginning of the sessions, they had virtually no material ready.

Well, at this point in their career, with the breakthroughs they made with the "Help!" album, it seems like The Beatles weren't ready to head back into the Carl Perkins' songbook to fill out an LP. They needed songs. They needed great songs...and they needed them now.

John and Paul would both say the task was "very impossible". But the great thing about true genius is that it's at its very best when things seems to be at their very worst. And so it was for The Beatles in putting together "Rubber Soul".

It was amazing that The Beatles came up with so many great songs so quickly...16 different titles in a month...almost a classic every other day. But it was absolutely dumbfounding that they got them all recorded by the deadline. But they did...and it wasn't a bunch of 20 hour sessions that made it happen either. (Though there was one of those at the finish line.)

With no time to spare, they spared no time in coming up with flawless performances immediately, it seemed, that matched the flawless material. The first song they'd cut on the first day of the sessions..."Run For Your Life"...took 5 takes. They wouldn't roll tape that many times on any other song they'd work on through the month. "If I Needed Someone" and "What Goes On"...one take. "Michelle", "We Can Work It Out", "Girl" and "Nowhere Man"...two takes. "Day Tripper", "In My Life" and "The Word"...three takes and on.

November 11th came and the album was done. And there was even a leftover ("12 Bar Original").

And, even in this writing and recording race against time, these weren't just songs...tracks that fleshed out an album. These were songs that began to flesh out Lennon, McCartney and Harrison's creative direction. There was folk, classical and blues influences to be heard. There were love songs, message songs. Songs that packed a lyrical punch or a punch line. All dashed off as if they were still cranking out hits for Billy J. Kramer and Cilla Black.

The Beatles would spend 5 times longer making "Sgt. Pepper" than "Rubber Soul" and, arguably, for as great as that landmark 1967 album was, they didn't come up with an album 5 times better.

We never noticed, of course. It was the next great album from The

Beatles...better than the one before, as they all were. But it was the group running at breakneck speed intending just to get an album done that wound up moving their career much farther ahead...and raising the bar...for themselves and everyone else at the same time.

There is that old line..."Do you want it right or do you want it now?" Well, The Beatles gave us both...Better than they ever did... better than anyone else ever did with "Rubber Soul". Most Memorable Moment #21.

#20 - THE 'GET BACK' SESSIONS

Like chocolate pizza and self-cleaning socks, "Get Back" was an idea that sounded great in theory, but wound up not working at all in practice. The Beatles were going to play live for the first time in years...A concert of new material that would become an album and, on the way they'd film the rehearsals for a TV special, too.

So, you'd have a concert, an album, a film and, subsequently, even a book.

It was a synergy soufflé. And it might have worked, too. But, again, without someone like Brian Epstein, The Beatles were trying to be jacks of all trades...writing the music, performing it, producing the film themselves, planning and promoting the concert and coordinating everything...ultimately proving to be masters of none of them...other than the music, of course.

You had several problems. First, the filming of the rehearsals. For one thing, the studio was The Beatles' private space. Nobody intruded. But, first, Yoko did, during the White Album sessions. Now, a film crew was going to be there. The Beatles...famously...had creative disagreements... loud ones throughout their years together. None of them affected their relationships until the last couple of years. But here, not only every note they played, but every word they said, would be recorded on film and tape. It was like working in your office...at a job you were beginning to hate...and doing it in front of a studio audience. In the case of The Beatles, it made an already deteriorating situation go downhill even faster.

Also, by then, The Beatles were used to working at night...late into the night often, but to satisfy the film crew...union demands and such...they had to work during the day. Originally, the rehearsals were supposed to happen on an ocean liner. But, the idea of the four of them being in such close quarters during such tense times didn't sit well with anyone, so they moved, instead, to a place where they worked during the shooting of "A Hard Day's Night" and "Help!", Twickenham Film Studios...a soundstage, not a recording studio. And, in the dead of winter, January of 1969, it was a cold soundstage, at that. And not a great environment for making music.

So, you had the wrong time and the wrong place and the wrong environment...The Beatles continually being watched...and filmed...by strangers.

In addition, The Beatles had finished the White Album little more than two months earlier. So, there was the question of where all these new songs for this live concert were going to come from just weeks after their last record had been completed. Beyond that, these guys worked themselves to the bone between '61 and '66. They didn't need to work that hard again. Most of them didn't want to. And they probably didn't need to get into a new project right then, the 'White Album' was still at the top of the charts and the "Yellow Submarine" soundtrack wasn't far behind. But Paul, fearing that too much time apart from each other would mean "out of sight, out of mind" and the band would eventually drift apart, pushed everyone into staying busy. And, instead of 'out of sight, out of mind', it became a case of familiarity breeding contempt.

Beyond that, "Get Back", as the album was to be called, was supposed to be, The Beatles "as nature intended;" and that comes from the promotional material done for the "Get Back" single. What that meant was the record was going to be 'unproduced' or, better stated, under produced. There wasn't supposed to be any additional instruments, no studio effects, not even any overdubbing or editing of the tracks after the fact, even though the band's skills to play spot on versions of songs had eroded, probably beyond what it was at the end of their days as a touring band. So, as they tried to play perfect versions of these new songs, invariably, somebody would make a mistake...and they'd have to start over again.

Ultimately, everything that could go wrong didn't, but it was certainly being set up as a situation where little could go right.

George had become disenchanted during the sessions for the 'White Album', but hoped for a better atmosphere with "Get Back"... but, as you could see in the film, he wound up arguing on camera with Paul and there was, apparently, an even worse argument with John that same day that the cameras didn't catch. When it became clear to him that the working situation wouldn't improve, George left...as in left the band.

A few days later, the four of them met and George dictated the terms for his return. No live show. So, the idea of playing at the Parthenon or on a ship with a huge audience on shore or in the Sahara desert went out the window. No more Twickenham. The rest of the sessions would happen at The Beatles' own studios at 3 Saville Row in London. (By the way, the Apple studios were another disaster. Designed by John's friend, Magic Alex Mardas...the guy who invented the 'Nothing Box'...literally a box with twelve lights on it that did nothing but suck electricity for five years...Honest to God...The studios in the basement of 3 Saville Row turned out to be a comedy electronics show...The sound console was built of particle board. Each of the eight tracks had their own little speaker. There were no provisions made for cables to be run from the studio into the control room...so they had to literally be run down the hall. Ultimately, the group had to borrow a remote truck from EMI to complete the recording.)

With the lack of a concert, that meant no new live album...so all the work The Beatles had been doing wound being preparation for a new studio album...and all the filming would be to document that now had no purpose. The idea of a TV special morphed into a movie...probably not coincidentally one that would complete the group's contract with United Artists.

It was with the move out of Twickenham that Harrison brought in Billy Preston, whom The Beatles knew as a 16 year old when he played the Star Club in Hamburg with Little Richard. He joined the band on "Get Back" and "Don't Let Me Down" and the mood in the studio lightened considerably.

They now needed a way to complete the film. And the idea of a live concert came up again. But the energy within the group had dropped to such a low level that they couldn't get themselves any further than the rooftop of their own building for their unplanned, but unforgettable 9 song set of tunes from the supposed forthcoming album. The Beatles ultimate live swan song.

Just getting through that whole month took enough out of The Beatles that none of them had the drive to sort through everything that had been recorded to piece together an album. One day, at Apple, John and Paul approached Glyn Johns, the engineer on the sessions, pointed to a stack of tapes on the floor...all of them from the just finished sessions...asked him if he wanted to assemble an album from them and that was it.

George Martin and he waded through hours of takes and mistakes of the same dozen or so songs and assembled an album full of false starts, sudden stops, screw-ups and break downs, guitar tuning and nose blowing...and I'm being serious. And, along the way, some simply marvelous music.

The "Get Back" album sounded like an hour of raw tape of The Beatles in the studio. It was marvelously honest. Perhaps too honest for The Beatles. Ultimately, probably because no one cared enough, the album went unreleased...and remains so...in that form...as you read this.

The band toyed with the idea of pulling some of the covers from the session and issuing a 'Beatles oldies' LP. That didn't happen either. Glyn Johns prepared an EP of covers from the sessions. That never saw the light of day either.

Instead, The Beatles went in and recorded a substitute LP for "Get Back"...That became "Abbey Road". Nice second choice.

But, with the film coming out and a soundtrack album expected, something had to be done. Phil Spector had just produced John's #1 single, "Instant Karma". George was in on those sessions and the two of them were impressed enough to ask Spector to work the "Get Back" tapes into an album.

With Spector on the scene, the idea of "as nature intended" disappeared. Tracks were lengthened, shortened, re-mixed. And, in a couple of cases, songs that were supposed to feature The Beatles alone in the studio had strings and brass and choruses added to them... most notably "The Long And Winding Road", done without Paul's permission or pleasure. That may not have driven Paul out of the band, but it certainly didn't help keep him there. "Get Back"...the title that described The Beatles' return to simpler music became "Let It Be"...the title that said it all...the end of The Beatles.

Decades later, at Paul's suggestion, the sessions were revisited and the tapes that were supposed to let us hear The Beatles as they actually made their music were taken apart, tracks reconstructed from pieces of different takes. Edited. Re-mixed. But, this time, the final product was as true...even if the means in getting there wasn't...to the original concept as could be thirty years after the fact.

So, the project that ended The Beatles and, as only they could do, produced two different #1 albums...30 years apart in the process...the "Get Back" sessions are The Beatles 20th Most Memorable Moment.

#19 - GEORGE MARTIN

Could it be that George Martin loved The Beatles...that mythic creation that the members of the band actually spoke of in the third person...more than the four guys in the group did? That he had more to do with shaping their sound, creating their 'to a cathedral's ceiling's' long list of hits and building their now unquestioned status as geniuses than those four geniuses themselves did?

There are jillions of talented people in this world. What they lack is someone to harness that talent, maximize it and translate it into work that could have the widest possible appeal. George Martin did that with The Beatles. And, if their everlasting success is any indication, no one has ever done a better of job of doing that for any other artist in any other realm.

He was more than their producer. He was their editor. Their collaborator. Even, if truth be told, their creative repairman. Here are just a small list of some of the things he did for...and with their music:

Starting at the beginning...

"Love Me Do"
It was Martin who decided to change who'd sing the solo vocal lines on "Love Me Do" from John to Paul, thus making McCartney the first Beatle 'lead singer' that people outside of a concert venue would hear.

"I Saw Her Standing There"
Not satisfied with how the final master began, Martin took the count in from Take 4 of "I Saw Her Standing There" and grafted it onto the released take 9.

"Please Please Me"
After initially working on the song as a ballad, Sir George told The Beatles to re-do the song, make it more upbeat, which the group did, turning it into their first #1.

"Rock And Roll Music"

Jerry Lee Lewis look out! Perhaps the most dominant part of the song...even beyond Lennon's vocal...which is saying a lot...is that boogie woogie piano throughout and, especially, at the finish. Played, obviously, by George Martin...I thought oboe was his instrument. (And I doubt that the Killer could do on the oboe what Sir George did there on the 88's.)

"Yesterday"

It was Martin's idea to add strings to "Yesterday" and, in the process, he turned the next beautiful Beatles' ballad into The Beatles first evergreen.

"In My Life"

After John asked him to write the instrumental break, Martin tried a version with an organ. Not satisfied with that, he wrote a Bach influenced piece that he tried to play on the piano, but couldn't play what he wrote fast enough, so he used verispeed...slowing the tape down so he could keep up. The result, of course, was that the piano sounded like a harpsichord...played by someone who's fingers worked fast enough to be a safe cracker...but who noticed. So, not only did he write the music, he came up with the studio trickery to get it recorded.

"Tomorrow Never Knows".

In the middle section of the song, Martin mixed tape loops playing on five different machines at one time...live. Technicians were using pencils within the loops to maintain the proper tension. At the end, it is Sir George on piano (again), this time playing the Looney Tunes theme. (And we got the joke, Mr. Martin.)

"Strawberry Fields Forever"

John thought the slow take (Take 7) was too slow and the fast take (Take 25) was too fast, but liked elements of each. Then he left it to Sir George to figure things out...which he would do. He adjusted the speeds of each and, somehow, they fell into the same key. (This guy should have gone to Vegas.) He edited out the pieces of each take to make the arrangement flow. And...bingo...that's how you create a miracle.

"Being For The Benefit Of Mr. Kite"

You thought it was just The Beatles whose random acts of insanity turned their music into gold? Looking for a way to make the song more ethereal, Sir George took tape of a calliope playing, cut it up, threw the pieces in the air and told engineer Geoff Emerick to reassemble them into a loop, so he could use it as part of the end of 'Mr. Kite'. You can't get much more random than that.

"A Day In The Life"
Lennon wanted the end of the song to sound like the end of the world...and George Martin gave it to him, writing that apocalyptic, atonal crescendo that finishes rock's most famous album with its most famous single note.

"Abbey Road"
Martin largely constructed the elements that would link together the song fragments that weren't finished and, in many of the cases, couldn't be finished and turned it into the most sophisticated work we would get from The Beatles...and, probably, anyone else in rock music.

Then, beyond The Beatles...

"Sentimental Journey"
Sir George's production somehow putting Ringo in the British Top 7 with an album made for grandmothers.

"Live & Let Die"
He would produce three McCartney albums, but his first work with his favorite student was a single that got to #1 and featured a trademark instrumental break which Martin composed but for which he never received credit.

"All Those Years Ago",
George had a hand in putting another Beatle at the top of the charts by himself...helping to produce this close as you could get reunion.

"Grow Old With Me"
When the "Lennon Anthology" came out, we got to hear this unfinished song as John wanted us to hear it...thanks to the arrangement and production of George Martin.

Then...The Beatles Again...

"The Beatles At The Hollywood Bowl"
The group never thought the recordings of those concerts sounded good enough to release. George Martin proved them wrong, laboring over the tapes...(They were recorded on a three track machine which, in 1977, was harder to find than Nixon supporters. One was found, but it was so old that it was quickly overheating. Martin brought his genius to bear again...coming up with the idea to have a vacuum cleaner run in reverse...blowing cold air on the deck while the tapes were being transferred to a 16 track machine.)...mixing the best of three concerts into one and coming up with the essential document of Beatlemania live and, if not one of the best performed in concert albums then, absolutely, one of the most exciting. (And it put the band back at #1 almost 8 years after it broke up. As we've said a lot so far, unprecedented.)

"Real Love"
Don't know if this actually happened, but, based on his unfailing skill in making the right choices regarding The Beatles, we'll mention it anyway. On the album version of The Beatles' last recording, John, Paul and George repeat the chorus as the song fades out and, on the final time, as those three Beatles finish singing, Ringo gives one last cymbal crash and The Beatles are done. Absolute genius. They walk off stage, as it were, together.

On the single version, you can hear George begin another guitar riff after that.

The difference? George Martin's name appears as "Executive Producer" on "Anthology 2". He gets no credit on the single.

And you could just imagine Martin being there at the mastering session for the album, hearing that last hit to the cymbal with the rest of the band finishing their vocal work and Sir George saying "That's where it should end...Right there." It does make you wonder if, even on the last studio work from the band...even though he didn't produce it...he still added his touch to give a perfect ending to The Beatles studio legacy.

"While My Guitar Gently Weeps"
The Beatles' "Love" version of the song for which Martin wrote a gorgeous string arrangement along with co-producing the latter-day Beatles' landmark (and he sadly, it seemed, said that that would be the

last score he'd ever write for The Beatles...and, sadder still is that he was probably right.)

And those were just some of his most obvious contributions to The Beatles' work...together and apart...through the years. We would need a calendar, not a clock to fit in everything else.

George Martin started working for EMI in 1950, as an assistant to the head of one of its labels, Parlophone. Within five years, he headed that label...part of his duties was finding new acts and also producing them. And, though he was a classically trained musician...on the oboe, as we said...he produced not only that but jazz, Broadway flavored pop, comedy records and, as early as 1957, rock and roll and worked with artists who ranged from Ella Fitzgerald to Sophia Loren to Peter Sellers to the British skiffle band, the Vipers. (And, in fact, hit #1 in America 6 years before his protégés did...producing Laurie London's stateside chart topper, "He's Got The Whole World In His Hands" in 1958.)

Truth be told, he gave The Beatles an audition as a courtesy to a friend and gave the band their contract...and not a particularly good one...only after Brian Epstein threatened to pull all EMI releases from his family's very successful music stores.

But, soon enough, he saw their talent, their drive and their intrinsic appeal as people. In terms of what he brought to the table, he showed, from his attention to detail so small as moving that count-in from "I Saw Her Standing There" from one take to another, how hard he'd work to get a record as close to perfection as possible. He was known as an innovator, even before he'd met The Beatles. His classical training proved to be an essential counterpoint to their backgrounds in rock and roll. He worked with The Beatles in the early days so that they could turn his ideas into reality in the studio and, as they developed as songwriters, and, really, song creators, Martin worked so that he would turn their ideas into reality. From the most sophisticated to the most outrageous sounds, what The Beatles heard in their heads, George Martin was able to let the entire world hear.

He would work with other acts...from Brian Epstein's collection of talent...Cilla Black, Gerry & the Pacemakers, Billy J. Kramer and later, with people like America, the Little River Band, Elton John, Jeff Beck...

all of whom had some of their greatest successes...creatively and/or commercially...with records he produced. But, as John, Paul, George and Ringo wound up doing their most memorable work together, so George Martin did his working with them.

In a sense, after the band's break up, he continued to work to build The Beatles' creative legacy while each of its members was busy working on his own. Working to tweak their sound, even for a re-package like "Rock & Roll Music"...where he re-mixed some of the tracks for that album to make them sound more contemporary. (And, by the way, he did that for free. EMI had planned to use twin track mono masters for the songs on the compilation. He stepped in...without asking for a nickel and put together the highest charting thematic package in rock history (and the first platinum album The Beatles would earn.) I guess that's what people mean by the term 'labor of love'. As we mentioned, 'Hollywood Bowl' was another example of that. John, Paul, George and Ringo couldn't have cared less about those decade old tapes, but George Martin did. He made sure that, regardless of what else may happen to The Beatles' legend, no one was going to be allowed to tinker with the music, as he produced the soundtrack for the far less than successful movie adaptation of 'Sgt. Pepper'. By the way, though the film flopped, the album from it hit the national Top 5 and produced three hit singles. And, of course, he shepherded the entire "Anthology" project... ultimately have 'aye' or 'nay' say over virtually every note of music The Beatles ever had committed to tape. He retired in 1996 after producing a Beatles' tribute album.

He retired again, a few years later, after producing Elton John' tribute to Princess Diana after her death, the updated "Candle In The Wind". But, ultimately, he could not leave music...especially the music of The Beatles...coming back again, in 2006, to produce "The Beatles Love" album. After that, his son Giles inherited the mantle and, with his work on "The Beatles Rock Band" and "The Beatles Live", it shows that the senior Martin not only produced genius level music, but genius level children, too. (And, by the way, knowing that he dropped by the sessions for these projects, it is impossible to think that he didn't, in some way, give some input that would make them work even better... So, Sir George's work with the band continues as he approaches 90.)

One regret may be that The Beatles, individually, didn't ask him to produce their work much more than they did. He certainly didn't need the work, but, often times, their solo music did. And part of the reason The Beatles' music on their own probably doesn't receive as much attention as it might is because George Martin didn't produce it.

And, if he feels as protective of everything The Beatles accomplished in the studio as they do, perhaps he has every right because his five decades worth of work with them proves, beyond doubt, that as phenomenally talented as they all were, The Beatles would never have become The Beatles without him. He was as much of a genius, a groundbreaker, an envelope pusher in his own way as The Beatles were. Maybe more so.

The group's 19th Most Memorable Moment is John, Paul, George and Ringo meeting the fifth Beatle...George Martin.

#18 - SHE LOVES YOU

The Beatles already had two straight #1 hits, but, with the release of "She Loves You" there were no longer any doubts about the phenomenon The Beatles had become in Britain. Of course, it was a spectacular record, full of energy, with an instantly catchy melody and an innovative story line...singing about a relationship in the third person. And, to be sure, that major sixth chord at the end of the song... something right out of Glenn Miller. George Martin thought that idea was corny, but, as smart as he was on his own, he was also smart enough to know when to let The Beatles talk him into something and this was one of those time. And, most importantly....that hook..."yeah, yeah, yeah". Prototypical element of what you need for a hit record. Never, never better done.

Believe it or not, it was inspired by Bobby Rydell's record, "Forget Him"...also a great record but it's hard to think of Rydell as someone who'd influence The Beatles' music. but, wherever it came from, the song absolutely took The Beatles to another level.

Again, as was the case at this point, John and Paul wrote the song together...somehow the exact date was remembered by someone...June 26th, 1963. They started writing it on a bus on the way to playing at the Majestic Ballroom, one of their stops on their 'Mersey Beat Showcase'... which featured The Beatles, Billy J Kramer and the Dakotas and Gerry and the Pacemakers, who, according to Mark Lewisohn, has the top three records in England at the time...got most of the song done in a hotel room in Newcastle-upon-Tyne before the show and finished it up at McCartney's home the next day.

The band recorded it on the 4th of July. Parlophone released it on August 23rd. Now, "From Me To You" had an incredible run on the charts. Seven weeks at #1, as we said. 12 weeks in the top ten overall. But "She Loves You" made it look like a mid-charter. It hit the British top ten at the end of August, hit #1 a week later and stayed there 'til the end of January of '64...21 weeks, including two different stays at #1 nearly two months apart. Chubby Checker did that with "The Twist"... but that record fell off the charts completely and was re-released 15 months later...still pretty impressive on Chubby's part. And it would spend more weeks in the top ten...nearly twice as many, in fact, as any other British Beatles 45. And no single from the group would spend as much time on the charts as "She Loves You" did...and it wasn't even close.

The record would be The Beatles first million seller and would become the biggest selling single in UK history...and would remain so for the next 15 years (overtaken, ironically enough, by Paul, a fragmentary version of Wings and "Mull Of Kintyre"). And, this is speculation on my part, but the overwhelming success of "She Loves You" is probably what led the BBC to give The Beatles their chance to appear on...and headline "Sunday Night At The London Palladium", which, of course, brought Beatlemania into millions of British homes for the first time.

And, on an even bigger scale, it was the success of "She Loves You" in Britain that made it impossible for EMI's American subsidiary, Capitol, to say "no" to The Beatles any longer, committing to pick up the option on the group's next single and promoting the hell out of it and setting up their explosion in the US weeks later.

But, apart from all that, the song's tag line..."Yeah, Yeah, Yeah"...sang 32 times in the song's 2:18, was one of the earliest and most obvious examples of the positivism the group preached, which is one of the little mentioned but unmistakable reasons for the half century long love affair the world has had with them. (By the way, Paul initially wanted that part of the song to be 'call and response'...He'd sing "She loves you", then John and George would answer with the "yeah, yeah, yeah's", but Lennon talked him out of it.)

It is such a touchstone for the band that its lyrics have been referenced in speeches by political leaders, in headlines praising other work from the group...even used briefly in the opening number of the Summer Olympics in London nearly 50 years later.

It would be the first song The Beatles would cross reference... with Lennon famously singing it during the long fade to "All You Need Is Love". And would be the rare title that would be crossed referenced by members of the group both while they were together and after...with Paul and Stevie Wonder singing the main line to the song near the end of "Tug Of War's, "What's That You're Doing"

So, for being the marvelous reason why they took over England and for being the reason why they became primed to take over America, "She Loves You" checks in as The Beatles 18th Most Memorable Moment.

#17 - PLEASE PLEASE ME (THE ALBUM)

It wasn't until recently that I began to appreciate the "Please Please Me" LP as more than just a great record. It was as groundbreaking in its own way as 'Sgt. Pepper' would be four years later. Up until then, albums by rock music artists...all of them...were secondary efforts to the singles they put out...if there was any effort put into them at all. The LP's consisted of the artist's most recent single, maybe his next one... maybe a couple of others that came out earlier but weren't hits, the 'B' sides from all of them and some other songs they cut that weren't thought to be good enough to put on either side of a single to fill out the record.

But George Martin wanted to do something different with The Beatles. His original intent for a first Beatles' album was to record them at the Cavern, but, as exciting as the atmosphere was there, the acoustics would never have allowed for a proper recording. So he decided instead to have The Beatles, basically, do an album in the studio that would approximate seeing The Beatles live. He and the group went over their extensive live set list and sequenced the album as if they were a planning a live 14 song set. Probably for the first time in rock history, an album's worth of music was recorded for the sole intent of being an album.

Then there was actually getting the chance to do an album. In early February of 1963, The Beatles were no longer nobodies, but they weren't yet somebodies...if you know what I mean. They had, to their credit, only one top 20 single..."Love Me Do" and "Please Please Me" had just reached the top ten. They were still, in essence, a local band... building a following beyond that, but nobody knew how far things would go. The brass at EMI took a chance though, and committed to an album for The Beatles...but they hedged their bets... giving the band just one day to record it. One day. 585 minutes in the studio. That's all they got, but that's all it took.

On Monday, February 11th, the meter started running. The band and Sir George had planned what songs to record...even what order in which to record them. Ten songs in ten hours. Seemed very doable.

The first session started at 10 AM...And there's that wall in front of you. The first song they tackled..."There's A Place"...wound up tackling them. It took 13 takes. Then came "I Saw Her Standing There". They made 11 passes at that one. All of a sudden, it's one o'clock and time for lunch...and one of the two sessions Sir George had originally scheduled was over...with only 2 songs done.

Back at 2:30 and they made better progress. "A Taste Of Honey" was done in 5 takes and "Do You Want To Know A Secret?" in 6. Then, they tried "Misery"...and tried and tried it. Such a basic song, yet it took The Beatles 11 takes to bring it home. And, as they did, it was time for dinner. 6 o'clock and the afternoon session was finished.

Luckily, George Martin was able to work in a third session, but The Beatles would have to record 5 more songs in about 3 hours...half the album. They went after "Hold Me Tight...spent 13 takes on it...and never came up with anything they wanted to use. (The version of the song that came out on "With The Beatles" was one that was re-recorded for that album.) Now, they had 2 hours to finish the album. Well, they finished "Anna" in 3 takes. "Chains" was banged out in 4. The version of "Boys" you hear on "Please Please Me" was the only time the band played it at Abbey Road...Perfect in one take. Amazing. They got "Baby It's You" done in 3. By then, it was 10 o'clock...at night. The third and last session was supposed to be over...and The Beatles were one song short of an album. "Twist & Shout" was left to be done... Intentionally put at the end of the set because he knew Lennon's voice would be shot after that. Well, it was already shot. John had been suffering from a cold...alternately sucking on cough drops and smoking cigarettes that day in the studio. Well, he took off his shirt, drank a swig of milk and let loose. Obviously, he nailed it. (There was a second take, but Martin's decision was right. Lennon gave whatever he had on the first take. Would still love to hear that second one though.)

The results? 30 weeks at #1 from the start of May '63 to the end of November...at a time when the top of the album charts in Britain were reserved for movie soundtracks and easy listening artists. And, speaking of #1, the "Please Please Me" album would spend nearly seven months there...hitting the top of the charts at the beginning of May, 1963 and staying there until the end of November. And, had "With The Beatles" not been released, "Please Please Me" would have remained #1 until the end of April, 1964...nearly one year straight as the most popular album in Britain. It hit the top ten for the first time at the beginning of April, 1963 and left it for the last time at the end of June, 1964...15 months later...64 weeks in the top ten. Even in the face of 'Sgt. Pepper' and "Abbey Road", "Please Please Me" remains the group's all time most popular LP in their homeland. For their efforts that day, The Beatles each received seven pounds, ten shillings...about $25 bucks...for the session fee. The album itself cost all of 400 pounds to produce. (The cover for 'Sgt. Pepper' cost 3000 pounds.)

Its impact? From then on, rock groups...the best of them, anyway... would record singles and they would record albums. Long form and short form works. In fact, The Beatles' next album, "With The Beatles" contained no singles. And that would lay the groundwork for the two being entirely separate creative entities...like "Rubber Soul" and 'Sgt. Pepper' and on.

And that success changed the thinking in the music industry. Until then, record company executives were satisfied getting money from their teenage customers $1 at a time...through the purchase of singles. But with the staggering success of "Please Please Me", they discovered they could start getting money from young people $3 at a time and, eventually, with the advent of the compact disc...Many more times than that. In essence, The Beatles with the "Please Please Me" album changed the entire business model of the record industry...which had been in place for about 50 years and set the stage about 25 years later for the virtual extinction of the 45 rpm record.

All that accomplished in a little less than 10 hours. And, altogether, that should be more than reason enough why the "Please Please Me" album is The Beatles 17th Most Memorable Moment.

#16 - THE CAVERN

Bill Harry, a real authority on The Beatles, referred to the Cavern as "the most famous club in the world" in the early and mid-sixties and, his own personal feelings aside, he's probably right.

The Cavern consisted of a small group of cellars built below warehouses in Liverpool. In World War II, they were used as air raid shelters, but, by the late 50's, they were empty. A man named Alan Sytner had been promoting jazz concerts in town, knew of an underground Parisian venue that had success bringing in musical acts turned the cellars into the Cavern. It offered trad jazz and, eventually, modern jazz and skiffle. The Beatles actually played skiffle there...as the Quarrymen in August, 1957 and got a criticism from the boss when they played music from Elvis.

The club struggled financially. Sytner sold out to his accountant, Ray McFall, who would eventually make the Cavern a rock and roll club. The group would first appear there as The Beatles in February of 1961 and, not long after, in a sense, they became that venue's house band...appearing there nearly 300 times...often twice a day. They would share the bill with heroes like Gene Vincent and Little Richard, as well as bands for whom they'd open the doors of success...people like the Hollies, the Searchers and Gerry & the Pacemakers. The Beatles would help the Cavern earn its reputation...and vice versa.

It offered only a small stage that barely had enough room for four Beatles. There were no curtains, no stage lights...just a row of 60 watt bulbs, if you can believe it. Also, no ventilation, no tables, no chairs and, as Beatle brain Mark Lewisohn said, "no room".

The Beatles were not only almost on top of one another, the crowd was almost on top of them. Those close quarters, though, only added to the kineticism of the venue. The Beatles on stage picking up the energy from the crowd right in front of them...and giving it back to them.

As The Beatles became known worldwide, so did the Cavern, TV news crews from around the globe came to do stories on it, so did magazines like Newsweek, Time and Life. Even a weekly radio show began being broadcast from there.

Eventually, McFall started representing artists himself. He bought the area next door, expanded the club and built a recording studio. But, he overextended himself financially and, not long after, declared bankruptcy. The club soon re-opened, but Liverpool city officials eventually decided the area around the Cavern was needed for an underground railway. And the Cavern became a parking garage.

Years later, the city...and some wise investors...saw the error of their ways. They understood that the Cavern was more than a club, a dance hall...It was history and turned the area into something of a living museum called Cavern Walks...complete with as accurate a recreation as possible of the original Cavern...even the use of some of the same bricks...honoring what has become one of the best remembered music venues in the world...and the band that made it so.

The Beatles really polished their act in Hamburg but it was at the Cavern where it paid off. The magnetism they projected, especially in such a small venue, drew everyone in. Word about them soon spread and, as a result, they quickly became the best known band in Liverpool, then in the North of England. London would follow, soon after the whole of England, then the US and the world.

The Cavern's importance to The Beatles can't be understated. If they found their mojo in Hamburg. They refined it...mainstreamed it at the Cavern. That was where they went from leather to sweaters to suits. They no longer smoked on stage or swore at their audiences. It was at the Cavern that they went from being the Rolling Stones to being The Beatles.

Brian Epstein would discover them there. Dick Rowe would give them their Decca audition based on his seeing them there. George Martin saw them there, too, and, when he did, he no doubt understood why Brian Epstein was so insistent on his giving them a recording contract. It's where London fell in love with them, where all of England saw them on television for the first time. John Lennon would spend his wedding night on the Cavern's stage. Pete Best spent his last night as a Beatle playing there...and Ringo Starr spent his first.

'Beatlemania', the term, may not have come along until October of 1963, but the mania itself started much earlier...and it started here. The Cavern. The Beatles 16th Most Memorable Moment.

#15 - ABBEY ROAD

With The Beatles' break up coming just months later, "Abbey Road" was the album that left the group's fans everywhere asking the never answered question, "What if?" If The Beatles had taken so great a musical step forward with this album, where would they have gone creatively had they stayed together?

"Abbey Road" was not as adventurous as 'Sgt. Pepper'...or even the 'White Album', but it was easily their most sophisticated work.

It began as something of an amends...to George Martin, to their fans, even to themselves and their own legacy. None of them, it seemed, wanted the haphazard recordings from "Get Back" to be the last thing people heard from The Beatles. And, everyone, tacitly, understood that The Beatles probably had only one more album left in them.

But what an album it was. The structure of "Abbey Road" resulted as a compromise between John and Paul. Lennon wanted an LP of individual songs...as The Beatles had done in the past. McCartney wanted the record to be something of a musical chain, one track linked to another with the entire work united by a recurring musical theme. A device used frequently in classical music and one suggested to The Beatles for this album by George Martin.

So side one...as originally released...goes track by track and side two is, more or less, one complete programme, linked, really, by a recurring riff...a series of arpeggios...first heard at the end of side one on John's "I Want You (She's So Heavy)".

And, honestly, both sides work extremely well. But the album showcases two Beatles primarily...George Harrison who may, with "Something" and "Here Comes The Sun", have written the album's two best songs. And McCartney, for his work with George Martin in assembling the 'huge medley' as they called it. And Ringo deserves a mention, too, for his continued growth as a songwriter, demonstrated by "Octopus's Garden".

Coming off their most undisciplined work (the 'Get Back'/'Let

It Be' debacle), The Beatles actually rehearsed the music they would be recording and, the infighting that plagued the group's previous two albums was kept to a minimum...perhaps because everyone knew they only had to survive these last sessions together. But, in fact, there was a more collaborative feel to this album than there had been to the 'White Album'...surprising because seldom during the sessions for "Abbey Road" were all four Beatles in the studio together. Some reports had Lennon less than fully involved in the album because of George Martin's siding with McCartney on the album's musical design. And, to be sure, his energy, by that time, was occasionally focused outside of The Beatles. But, with songs like "Come Together" and "Because", John could hardly be considered a guest star.

It was done in a month...Amazing. 'Pepper' and the White Album took five times as long. Maybe the four of them understood that, if they committed to that much time together, the album would never have been completed. As it turns out, 30 days was plenty of time.

"Abbey Road" showed the world how The Beatles had grown up, sadly, as they had grown apart. Starting off by inviting us to "Come Together", through Harrison's beautiful "Something" and Maxwell Edison wielding his 'silver hammer', weaving its way through a maze of unfinished tunes that worked better in the context of following one another anyway and finishing things with "The End", the four of them walking out the door by restating their mantra one last time...the simple equation of life...love given equals love taken. Paul talking about 'instant karma' months before John did.

"Abbey Road" would spend 15 weeks as America's #1 album among the national trade magazines...equaling 'Sgt. Pepper' for that honor and it would become the group's bestselling album...which only led to another "What if"? "What new musical heights would their next album have scaled had The Beatles not broken up?" We would never get that question answered, of course, but, after giving us a creation like "Abbey Road", did we really have the right to ask for more?

There is that old show business expression about 'always leaving the audience asking for more. It was never better exemplified than The Beatles last work together.

For showing that, to the end, The Beatles kept searching for a limit to their talents...and were unable to find it...with "Abbey Road" being proof. The Beatles' last album is the group's 15th Most Memorable Moment.

#14 - STRAWBERRY FIELDS FOREVER

You know we're getting closer to the top, because each one of these items becomes more and more significant.

"Strawberry Fields Forever" was just such a complete break from the past...in every way. First the lyrics: "No one I think is in my tree. I mean he must be high or low. That is you can't, you know, tune in but it's all right. I mean, I think it's not too bad". Well, need I say more? At this point in his career, Dylan could be indecipherable. In 'Strawberry Fields', Lennon was incoherent. If he wasn't stoned when he wrote it, he should have been. If he wasn't stoned when he sang it, it sounded like he was. But, for that, there's an explanation apart from Lennon's state of sobriety at the time. And it involves another near miracle happening to The Beatles.

"Strawberry Fields Forever" started its life as a folk song...John on guitar. It grew, with the band's involvement into a more fully arranged, but still very innocent sounding tune. But John was not satisfied with the song done that way.

George Martin re-did the arrangement, brought in trumpets and cellos and the new version of the song was done in almost a march cadence...kept in time by the pounding of Ringo's drums.

Ultimately, John wouldn't settle for either version of the song, but he had a thought...put them together. A great idea, George Martin told him...except for the fact that they're in different tempos and different keys. "Well", Lennon replied, "you can fix that". And he walked off.

But fix it, he did. He slowed down the fast one and sped up the slow one and, amazingly, somehow they fell into the same key. He edited John's vocal...so that it fit within the new 'arrangement' of the tune, took elements from each of these so different versions of the song, pieced them together, adding backwards masking throughout and a coda that featured forward and backward masking on top of one another...That coda will sound the same whether you play it backwards or forwards. In the end, he came up with a master take that became a record absolutely unique among rock music singles. A track that, even today, couldn't be performed spot on live...even if John were still with us...simply because his actual vocal was so drastically affected by verispeed...the studio technique that changes how fast or slow a tape would playback. (That's why he sounded drugged. It was a technologically induced high.)

The song, surprisingly today maybe, hit the American top ten and shared #1 as a double 'A' side in England with "Penny Lane". It is probably...easily, probably...the most unorthodox piece of music ever to hit the top ten. Then and now. The Beatles here demonstrating, perhaps, one of their greatest gifts...moving further and further out, yet never so far that they'd be out of the range of their audience.

It broke every convention that had existed on pop music singles...since the days of the 78...In terms of lyrics...absolutely absurdist rhetoric. The kind of stuff you'd hear from the guy next to you at the bar at 1:45 AM. Melody? Nowhere near the bright, poppish stuff we'd always gotten from The Beatles and everyone on Top 40 radio. Arrangement? Strings playing soft, brass playing loud. Unheard of. Production? have you ever heard a record that sounded like that before? Performance? 'SFF' made John's vocal on the coda of "Rain" make him sound like a teetotaler. Even its length. 'Strawberry Fields' was the first Beatles song to go longer than four minutes and, as far as I can remember...only Dylan, with "Like A Rolling Stone" and Marty Robbins' "El Paso" had singles which broke the four minute barrier before it.

'Strawberry Fields' would be the first song worked on for the album that would become 'Sgt. Pepper' and the only reason it wasn't included on the LP was because EMI had pressured George Martin and The Beatles for two sides of a new single. (And it has been one of Sir George's greatest creative regrets ever since.) But, in being issued on a 45, it really served a greater purpose. It got everyone ready for the music that would come from The Beatles...and everyone else...within the coming months. And it opened the door for more radical music, from people like Jimi Hendrix and Janis Joplin, to be played on Top 40 stations next to people like Petula Clark and the Cowsills.

For being such a total departure...in so many ways from anything anyone had ever heard before playing at 45 rpm...and yet for still sounding like an unforgettably hit single, "Strawberry Fields Forever" is The Beatles 14th Most Memorable Moment.

#13 - I WANT TO HOLD YOUR HAND

The Beatles took over the world's stage in 1964 and "I Want To Hold Your Hand" was the spotlight. Supposedly, the song was tailored for the American audience. Maybe a little more R & B flavored with the lyrics, perhaps, dumbed down a bit to go along with what else was happening musically over here. (Songs like "My Boyfriend's Back", "It's My Party" and "Sugar Shack" all hit #1 in the months before The Beatles kicked things loose here and none of those titles had lyrics that could be called intellectually stimulating.)

With the success that had been building for The Beatles in Britain (from "Please Please Me" to "From Me To You" to "She Loves You"... each a progressively bigger #1), Capitol Records, EMI's subsidiary in America, couldn't ignore what was happening abroad and finally chose to release a Beatles' record in the US themselves and Brian Epstein talked the company into spending $40,000...an enormous amount then...to promote the single and the group.

In retrospect, that may not have been necessary.

A US release date was set for January 11th. By then, though, they had become so popular in England that CBS sent a film crew to shoot footage of one of their concerts. It was scheduled to be broadcast on the CBS Evening News on December 10th, 1963.

A 15 year old named Marsha Albert saw the broadcast, became a fan and, later, heard that The Beatles had a new record out in England. And, in fact, "I Want To Hold Your Hand" came out in Great Britain four weeks before it did in the US. She called Carroll James, a disc jockey at WWDC in Washington and asked him to play it. Well, of course, seeing it wasn't going to be released in the US for a month, he didn't have it.

He did, however, have a friend who was a stewardess for B O A C and he asked her to bring him a copy from England. She did. He started playing the record on December 17th...the request lines went mad.

Capitol Records had an injunction issued for him to stop airing the song. He ignored the injunction. James had friends on the air in other markets. They heard about the response to the record and asked him to send them a tape of it. Soon stations in Chicago and St. Louis are playing the tune. Well, as far as I know, you can't stop an earthquake.

But, apparently, you can schedule it to happen sooner. Capitol had no choice but to move the release date for "I Want To Hold Your Hand" up to December 26th. The record came out and sold 1/4 of a million copies in its first three days in the stores. It was selling 10,000 copies an hour...an hour...in New York City. The demand for the single was so great that Capitol had to ask RCA and Columbia to help them press enough copies.

As they touched down in the US for the first time, "I Want To Hold Your Hand" had reached the top spot in Cashbox Magazine, keeping the promise The Beatles made to themselves about not coming to America until they had a #1 here. It would stay there for two months and become the #1 record of 1964. Ultimately, at 15 million copies, it would be the biggest selling single worldwide to come from Britain.

It wasn't as lyrically clever as "Please Please Me, " as musically adventurous as "From Me To You", as catchy as "She Loves You". But sometimes, like the guy elected President doesn't appear to be the best person for the job and winds up as one of our best leaders, "I Want To Hold Your Hand" performed, as The Beatles would, better than the sum total of its individual elements.

Maybe "I Want To Hold Your Hand" was the right record to break The Beatles in the US. Or maybe it was just the right time. Whatever the reason it was that record's destiny. After "I Want To Hold Your Hand" hit here, everything changed...The Beatles lives...their careers, our tastes in music, our culture, priorities and values...everything. It not only launched The Beatles. It launched the Stones and the Dave Clark Five. The Hermits and the Yardbirds. Zeppelin and Elton John. Ozzy Osborne and Dusty Springfield. The Police and the Clash. And three generations...so far...of contemporary music performers from Britain.

For lighting the fuse that didn't just cause an explosion but set off a half century long minefield, "I Want To Hold Your Hand" is The Beatles 13th Most Memorable Moment.

#12 - PLEASE PLEASE ME

Even after "Love Me Do", The Beatles were still just a local Liverpool band with one minor hit. Of course, that label changed when the group released "Please Please Me".

That wasn't how George Martin thought it was going to happen. He was all ready to release the group's version of "How Do You Do It?"...a tune as lightweight as tissue...as the follow up to "Love Me Do". The group protested, insisting that they wanted their music...their singles, at least, to be self-written. And their choice for their second single was John's "Please Please Me".

Originally conceived as a big ballad like Roy Orbison would sing, the tune, as it was, wasn't working as they ran through it at Abbey Road. In fact, George Martin called it "a very dreary song". He suggested that they re-work it from a ballad into a rocker. It was one of the first times George Martin, while working with The Beatles, used the studio as a classroom. And it's not often that, in a teaching environment, you have one genius teaching four others. Martin, of course, turned out to be a marvelous instructor and The Beatles were great students. And this was probably the first example of that.

They not only made it more up-tempo. They added answer vocals in the chorus and harmonies throughout. And the work paid off. After they recorded the new version, Martin, showing he was as great a prophet as he was a producer, went on the talkback and told them they'd just recorded their first #1.

The song was an incredible leap ahead musically, strong melodically and gave the first sign of the lyrical cleverness to be found in so much of The Beatles' music thereafter. The inspiration for that coming to John, from an old favorite of his mother's...a 1932 hit from Bing Crosby called "Please", which featured the line, "Please lend your little ear to my pleas".

Within four weeks, the record was in the top ten...and it started a streak of new Beatles' single releases each hitting the British top ten that continues today. Three weeks later, it was #1, as Sir George predicted. And that started a string of 19 straight #1 singles for them in their homeland. No other artist was able to garner even half that many. It would spend three weeks at the top in one British chart, 9 weeks in the top ten in another. Modest by Beatles standards, but this was one Beatle chart topper that sold on the strength of the record alone. People bought it not because of The Beatles' name, but because of The Beatles' work.

And "Please Please Me" was not only groundbreaking for The Beatles, it was also door opening. Once they had that #1 under their collective belts, the group found themselves becoming virtual regulars on British radio and TV...appearing virtually weekly on BBC radio...(51 appearances there in 1963) and 38 national TV appearances. And it brought better bookings at bigger venues for more money...probably something that happens with any #1 record for any artist, but this, of course, wasn't any #1 record and The Beatles weren't any group of artists. And everything that happened because of the success of "Please Please Me", of course, would only fuel the flames that would follow with "From Me To You", "She Loves You" and "I Want To Hold Your Hand".

Here in the US, "Please Please Me" had the honor of being the first American Beatles single...and the first American Beatles flop. It never charted nationally...first time around (February 25, 1963...its initial release date here) and sold only 7,300 copies for Vee Jay (though it did hit the top 40 in Chicago thanks to legendary DJ 'the Wild I-tralian' Dick Biondi playing it on WLS.) George Martin never said anything about this being the record that would break the group in America...and he was right about that, too. But it wasn't a case of The Beatles not being ready for America. Just the opposite.

"Please Please Me" might be the prototypical early Beatles record...lock tight with a beat that drives you like a limo, and lyrics that have you using your head while the rest of the record has you using your feet. It got them to #1 first. A position they have seldom had to relinquish. The power and polish of the record got people...from fans to critics to record company execs to take them seriously and it started a momentum that hasn't stopped...five decades later. Whatever else came after, "Please Please Me" came first. And, for that, "Please Please Me" is The Beatles 12th Most Memorable Moment.

#11 - REVOLVER

I guess, today, they'd call it 'recharging your batteries' or 'getting away from it all'. We all know how a vacation refreshes us. Renews our energy. (Or is supposed to.) Gives us a fresh perspective, new ideas. And makes some of us actually look forward to going back to work... OK, that's a lie. Anyway, that's what 1966 promised for The Beatles. And, in their case, it turned out to be no lie at all.

After three grueling years under the constant pressure and spotlight of fame...McDonald's French Fries aren't under such heat... The Beatles finally were able to reclaim some of their personal and professional lives. In 1966, they made no movies. (There were plans to make a third one...a comedy/western called "A Talent For Loving" was considered, but never progressed beyond talk.) There were no more performances on BBC radio...only occasional interviews. Same with BBC TV. They no longer wanted/needed to appear on national media when they had a new record out. Instead, they would perform it in front of a movie camera...or do a conceptual piece to the song...and, inadvertently, created (or re-created) the music video. After their last tour of Britain finished in mid-December, 1965, The Beatles, basically, had 4 months off. They would not tour until late in the Summer.

Their only place of business, if you will, was the recording studio... and, even then, not until early Spring. They had the time to find new things to write about and new ways to write about them. Then, with nothing else on the docket, they were able to labor over those ideas, allow inspiration to happen and then, follow that until their ideas were realized. Over the two plus months that it took to record "Revolver", the band began to find the opportunity to go down musical roads they'd never taken before...freed from the days...as the "Help!" album did for them...of writing only boy-girl songs in a strictly pop rock idiom...played just by The Beatles (and, sometimes, George Martin) themselves. As it turned out, the roads that no one had taken before...certainly no one in rock music.

Coming off "Help!"...even "Rubber Soul"..."Revolver" was a combination shock and revelation. By this time, with the anticipation of a new Beatles' album, we knew we were going to get something great, but "Revolver" tore up the contract. Even the people who best recognized and understood their genius had to be delightedly dumbfounded by this incredibly innovative departure. For all the progression that could be heard in The Beatles work to that point... single to single and album to album, they would never before or again experience such an extraordinary (and I'm looking for more synonyms for the word 'incredible' because I think I'll be using every one of them here) broadening of their own musical horizons and come up with work that demonstrated such an instant ability to excel in them.

There was baroque, Indian, big band, country, psychedelic and straight ahead rock...all side by side. Songs about a doctor who drugs his patients, a lonely woman's sad death, the tax collector who wants to make sure he gets the pennies on your eyes, a trip on a yellow submarine, some young woman who claims to know what it's like to be dead. And sounds. Such new, wonderful, incredible sounds. George's somnambulant backwards guitar on "I'm Only Sleeping", the French horn on "For No One", the sitars and tambouras on "Love You To" and the carnival of experimentation on "Tomorrow Never Knows". Far, far stretches even from "In My Life", "Michelle" and "Think For Yourself".

From the start of their career, The Beatles never wanted to just be the biggest band. They wanted to be the best, knowing that, if they could do that, they would be the biggest. The core of their definition to become 'the best' seems to have meant that they were always 'getting better' (to quote their own song title). But it's one thing to find and follow your own creative muse. It's quite another to do that...and to do it to the degree that The Beatles did...and still have your audience stay with you. That, maybe, was the greatest aspect of The Beatles' genius. They could enjoy continued massive commercial success and amazing artistic growth at the same time without compromising either. Really a singular accomplishment.

They made great, progressive music throughout the album, but it still had a hit single on it..."Yellow Submarine/Eleanor Rigby". (Really, two if you count "Got To Get You Into My Life's post-break up success.) And they could have had 8 or 9. Regardless of how the album challenged what pop music could say, how it could be said and the music and production that would be the vehicles through which it would be said... The Beatles still, on every track, employed the basic construct of writing a great pop song...beat, melody, hook...and got it done in three minutes (and, by then, The Beatles had even stretched out that time limit by a full 60 seconds).

It went to #1 everywhere. But, of course, every Beatles album went to #1 everywhere.

It was not as trippy as 'Pepper'. Not as wide ranging as the 'White Album'. Not polished as "Abbey Road". But John, Paul and George...who, for the only time, got three of his tunes on a single Beatles' LP...never... collectively...wrote a better group of songs. It would be the perfect storm of The Beatles' experimentation meeting their ability to write great, commercial music. "Revolver" was The Beatles' greatest creative leap forward and, ultimately, with decades to consider and reconsider this, their greatest album.

Ultimately, "Revolver" will be remembered for its unprecedented inventiveness in every way without compromising its accessibility, and for breaking more new musical ground than, probably, any other rock album...from The Beatles...from anybody. Probably from any album of any kind...ever did.

For being their greatest collective work...and that's saying a lot..."Revolver" is The Beatles 11th Most Memorable Moment.

#10 - PAUL McCARTNEY LEAVES THE BEATLES

1969 seemed like another year like every other year for The Beatles. Four best friends making great new music that continually went in new directions. They would start the year working on the "Get Back" album. The "Get Back" single would hit in Spring. Quickly thereafter, they'd be back on the charts with "The Ballad Of John & Yoko". John came out with "Give Peace A Chance", but he'd already done those nonsense albums with Yoko. At least that was a good record. By the end of the year, the band was back at the top of the charts again with "Abbey Road", "Something" and "Come Together". They never sounded better and all was right with the world. Or, so it seemed.

But, before the year ended...before "Something" got to #1, in fact... John released a Plastic Ono Band follow up to "Give Peace A Chance"... "Cold Turkey". This was a formal studio recording. A real song... harrowing as it sounded. Not the gibberish he'd done with his soon to be wife. Not a movie soundtrack like Paul and George had already done. More than that, though, flags were raised when you looked at the record's label. The tune was credited to 'John Lennon'...not to 'Lennon/McCartney'. It would be the first time in his professional life where John would take sole credit for writing a song. Hmmm. It made you wonder.

By early February, The Beatles prodigies, Badfinger, were headed for the top ten with "Come & Get It", a song from Ringo's film, "The Magic Christian". When you got that record, you found out that it was written by 'Paul McCartney'...again a solo credit where you would expect credits for both he and John. Now, you could write that one off seeing that Paul had already written music for a film ("Love In The Open Air" for "The Family Way") himself...but you still had to begin wondering what was going on. Then John came out with "Instant Karma". Again, solo single, solo writing credit...and this one was a hit. It sounded like a record he'd do with The Beatles...only he did this one without them (save George on 'lead guitar' which was buried somewhere in the avalanche of Phil Spector's production.)

Within weeks, the world would, indeed, find out 'what goes on'. The Beatles were breaking up...ironically, as the "Let It Be" single hit #1 in America. (This stuff would be such great literature, if it weren't all true.) And the bearer of the bad news was Paul McCartney.

The Beatles' fall probably began with their rise. The Beatles worked like hell to establish themselves. Worked like hell to maintain their success. Finally, by the mid 60's, they could begin to take time off... Each began living his own life, meeting someone they loved and would marry, developing his own interests, exploring his own talents...without the others. Then, Brian Epstein died. The Beatles made the ill-considered decision to manage their own careers, the show business equivalent of trying to read a map and drive a car at the same time.

McCartney volunteers himself to direct the group's career... unintentionally positioning himself as a superior among equals. So now the others, who had to deal with Paul's tendency to be overbearing in the studio, had to deal with it in every other aspect of their relationship, too.

But it wasn't all Paul...by far. By early 1968, Yoko Ono had become very much the fifth wheel...and her presence often made it a bumpy ride. The Beatles started Apple as a well intentioned tax shelter, but the financial hemorrhaging that soon plagued the company added to the stress within the band. The curse of ever growing expectations from the world...which The Beatles always seemed to exceed from project to project...nonetheless put continuing greater pressure on the band. By the time they recorded the 'White Album', the independence they had found in their lives began to follow them into the studio and, within a year after the amazing collective triumph of 'Sgt. Pepper', individual Beatles began to care more about their own songs than the group's work as a whole. The creative disputes, always a part of The Beatles' artistic process were now getting louder and more personal. George was getting tired of being treated as a second level member of the band. Then came "Get Back", the rock and roll progenitor of "Survivor"...only here, ultimately, everybody voted themselves off the island.

Beyond the other tensions going on, everyone was writing so much wonderful music that everybody was having great songs left off of Beatles' albums. (And they proved that with all the great tunes they threw out the window on the way down the road...songs like "Art Of Dying", "Junk", "Gimme Some Truth", "All Things Must Pass", "Every Night", "Jealous Guy"...written, apparently, before John was not jealous...just a "Child Of Nature"...the song's original title and story line. I'd keep going, but I think I already closed the sale.)

The tensions grew worse. Somehow, the band agreed to a verbal ceasefire long enough to complete one of their finest albums..."Abbey Road". When the LP was done, Lennon told the others that he was leaving the band...verbalizing the inevitable. The Beatles were done.

Each of the four agreed that the end of the group will go unannounced. The financial situation at Apple continued to grow worse. John reasserted himself, bringing in Allen Klein to run things...over Paul's objection. Lennon and Harrison brought in Phil Spector to do something with the "Get Back" tapes in order to have an album ready by the time the "Let It Be" movie was released.

In the process of preparing the pseudo-soundtrack, Spector slathered "The Long & Winding Road" with strings, brass and a chorus without Paul's knowledge or consent and McCartney was livid. Instead of a Beatle getting angry over not having his songs recorded, now a member of the band was angry over what happened to one of his songs after it was recorded.

Early in 1970, Klein sanctioned the release of "The Beatles Again/Hey Jude"...a collection of supposedly hard to find singles. Ringo had finished his album of standards. The "Let It Be" film and album were in the queue...and so was Paul's first solo LP. As Lennon would say there was a lot of product coming out. Weeks before "McCartney" was to come out, Ringo went to see Paul, asking him to move back the release of his (Paul's) album, so as not to conflict with "Let It Be". Paul refused, flew into a rage and sent Ringo on his way. (Ultimately, the LP's from the band and Starr would be delayed to placate McCartney.)

When his LP did come out, Paul violated the band's tacit agreement and announced that he'd left The Beatles (and, worse, on the promo copies of the album, he included a 'self-interview' where he damned The Beatles...and other guys in it...with faint praise. With this, he had put The Beatles problems in print.)

Had the album come out with no announcement, the situation may have been salvageable. But with McCartney breaking the band's trust publicly and doing so apparently only to promote his own solo album... which still seems remarkably self-serving (I mean, what other reason could there have been for him doing it?), he further alienated the band.

By the end of 1970, he decided to take the other Beatles to court to end their partnership, giving the world the chance to now hear The Beatles throw insults at one another in public and causing a division among the members of the band that took decades to heal.

As you could see, it took a lot to make four guys who so joyfully made music together for so long break up so bitterly, but, somehow, it happened. The Beatles found their own way to do so many one-of-a-kind things in music and this, unfortunately, was one more of them.

And all that talk of "All You Need Is Love" and "Can't Buy Me Love" went out the window as the group fought over position, pounds sterling and power. All of it made The Beatles seem like hypocrites...and to the idealistic generation they raised, there could be no greater sin. And it didn't have to happen.

As we said, Paul didn't have to say a word...other than to sell a few more pieces of his own vinyl. He could have put the album out, not commented on the band's then-current state...or its future, as John had done with "Live Peace In Toronto" and George would do with "Wonderwall". When those albums came out, nobody gave any thought to The Beatles breaking up. It was just more music coming from the band.

Had McCartney kept his word and everyone would have been allowed to go their own way, the situation would have had time to simmer and, maybe, cool off completely. Maybe, after some reflection, the four of them would have seen what each contributed to the band's problems...and how much each contributed to each other's lives. Maybe... and it might have taken years...they would have gotten back together. Maybe not. There still would have been the financial issues to deal with if that were the case. And, had that proceeded, we would have found out that The Beatles had, indeed, stopped working together permanently. But, even if that were the case, it would have, in all likelihood, come long after the fact. The anger among them would have died down and, probably, they would all have been more circumspect in talking about the band and the best friends they had in it.

To millions of people around the world, rather than February 2nd, 1959...when the plane carrying Buddy Holly, Ritchie Valens and the Big

Bopper crashed, April 10th 1970 is the real day the music died.

Paul McCartney, the one member of the band who worked obsessively, longer and harder, and was willing to go to any length to keep The Beatles together would, ironically enough, be the one who, when he believed there could be no turning back, was equally obsessed...now to go to any length to break them apart. His actions, in the environment in which they happened, turned the fairy tale story of The Beatles into "Humpty Dumpty".

Paul's leaving The Beatles is the group's 10th Most Memorable Moment.

#9 - REAL LOVE

Maybe the most surprising entry on our list. It certainly raised a few eyebrows and a few voices. But, with every model of The Beatles 50 Most Memorable Moments that we came up with, "Real Love" was right there, right near the top. Now, being the last real Beatles record itself might have gotten it a place on our Top 50, but let me explain why "Real Love" is so significant in the group's story.

We just talked about The Beatles' break-up, but we didn't mention how it affected the group's fans...maybe even the entire world. Probably from the day Paul made his announcement about his leaving the band, thousands...millions of people asked them, pleaded with them, prayed for The Beatles to get together again. Honestly, and I mean this with all the respect in the world, quite possibly, next to the return of Jesus Christ, there was no second coming as anticipated as one from The Beatles.

But something always got in the way...There were the personal and business disputes in the early 70's. Then Paul's drug bust, which kept him out of America while John's deportation case kept him here. Then John left music to raise Sean. Then, tragically, came John's murder. But even after that, people still clamored for the remaining Beatles to work together...The world's passion for The Beatles' return would never end. Did you ever ask yourself why?

Yes, they made great, wonderful, innovative, unforgettable music. Incomparable, but still, as John would say, they were only a rock band. And, yes, they touched us in ways emotionally we probably can't even define. But it's more than that, too. When they broke up, so bitterly, so publicly in such a petty manner over their money and their egos, it put the lie to everything they had preached obviously, subtly...intentionally or not...in all their work.

For the generation of fans who grew up with them and the generations around before and after who grew to love them, The Beatles inspired us, shaped our ideals, gave us hope. They, invariably, made us feel better about ourselves and the world around us.

And yet, there they were. Going to extraordinary lengths to show us they couldn't practice what they preached. The world...at least the world of their fans was crestfallen. Was what they told us a lie? Was everything they said to us just so much fiction? If we can't believe in these musical parables The Beatles gave us...that made us feel so good... then what, in this otherwise cynical, selfish, dangerous world in which we're living, can we believe in? So the world hoped and begged for The Beatles to come back just one more time to prove that we hadn't wasted our faith in them...and that, in fact, what they preached was right.

Finally, 25 years after they'd broken up, they settled all their differences and the world was finally going to get new music from The Beatles. In those years apart, the myth regarding the band only grew. Remember, they left us with "Abbey Road", another giant creative leap forward. The peak of their musical sophistication.

In their years together, they seemed infallible, at least musically. We never heard The Beatles' bad choices. Those were saved for their solo years...when they had to do everything themselves and no longer had each other as impeccable sounding boards for their ideas...which only made the group look even more perfect in comparison.

Finally, their 'first new record in 25 years' came out, heavily promoted and eagerly awaited..."Free As A Bird". Too long, too grungy, too slow. Worse still, John's vocal sounded like it was coming off a tape rather than from his being in the studio with the others. (I will never understand how the remaining members of the band...brilliant as they were...didn't 'dirty up' Paul and George's solos...so they would sound just like John did.) The result was that "Free As A Bird" sounded like a dead man singing his own dirge.

To many fans, this was no Beatles reunion...sonically, creatively, even spiritually. Had Lennon brought that song to the band when they were still together, it would never have been considered for release as a single. For the first time, at least in terms of their music, The Beatles together made a mistake.

And fans had to wonder whether too much time had passed, if the sometimes faulty judgment they'd shown on their own had followed them back to the group...if The Beatles were now (and, maybe always were) mere musical mortals. Maybe it was just a 7 year long lucky streak that they chose to break themselves.

If The Beatles were ever going to recreate what they destroyed so many years before, they had only one more chance. The second...and last...reunion record. "Real Love".

It would come at the end of the second night of The Beatles Anthology. From the opening notes on that cheesy sounding piano, the fans of The Beatles recognized that very familiar sound. Something that hadn't been heard in 25 years and yet, was still unmistakable.

In fact, it was a Beatles highlight reel. A positive, upbeat, melodic song about love...catchy as hell...full of those lush Beatle harmonies and Paul's bass, George's guitar, Ringo's drums. John sounded like he was there in the studio with the others...thanks, in part, to one last Beatles miracle...Paul mimicking John's voice as a shadow vocal.

The Beatles had done it! Found a way to make one more perfect record...and do it with a dead man singing lead.

But more than that, the "Real Love" video is a part of the reason why the song is in our top ten. It is not as technically dazzling than the "Free As A Bird" video, but it is far more emotionally powerful. Early on, there's a shot from "Let It Be" with John in front of a mike. He finishes singing a line and begins mugging and it looks to all the world like he'd just sung a line from "Real Love". Again, dead man singing lead.

Later, there's a long shot of Paul and George giving each other a long hug. Any reason to think these guys were still at odds with one another? And, finally, near the end of the tune, there are two shots, one after the other...one of John strumming his guitar and smiling, then looking to his right. At that point, there's a cut to Paul, George and Ringo...arm in arm, smiling, too. The closest we could come to seeing the four of them together, having fun again.

But what those shots really said was, "Hey, you know all that stuff our music was about...all that hope, all those ideals...that we pretty much trashed for years later. Well, we've reconsidered things. And we really do believe all that stuff, we should never have stopped believing it and we hope you still believe it, too. And, with that, the 'myth' was re-positioned. All the idealism..."don't worship materialism", "be there for your friends", "believe in a better tomorrow" and, of course, "love one another"...all back in place. That 60's ethos...built on peace, justice... and, yeah, love...re-endorsed by the guys who wrote and delivered the gospel on it.

Damage...25 years worth...undone in just under four minutes. That's why "Real Love"...neglected as it is...is so vital to The Beatles story.

I talked to a psychologist friend of mine a while back...about The Beatles' reunion. He mentioned how guys, especially, in their fifties who'd been successful earlier in life want to go back to do again...just once...what they used to do so well...to prove to themselves that they could still do it. I asked him if he thought the reason why they did "Real Love" after "Free As A Bird" was because The Beatles felt, on some level, they hadn't done that...recaptured their magic...first time out. And he said, "yes". And I asked him if he thought the reason why they didn't finish the other demos Yoko gave them was because, with "Real Love" they'd accomplished what they'd set out to do. And he said "yes" again.

Maybe they gave us a clue to that at the end of "Real Love"...when, as John, Paul and George finish singing, Ringo gives a last cymbal crash. The Beatles finishing the song together and, in essence, walking off the stage together one last time.

"Real Love" was the first choice to be the band's first new record in a quarter century but technical limitations...and the inability to overcome them kept The Beatles from working on it until a year later. Nevertheless, the song charted as high as some of their biggest singles in England.

It hit the top ten in America, giving them a span of more than 30 years between their first and last top tens in Cashbox...the longest such streak in that magazine's long history. It earned a gold record in America faster than many of the group's earlier hits and made The Beatles the third oldest artists...behind Lawrence Welk and Louis Armstrong...to earn a gold single.

After they broke up, hearing one more last great track and knowing that they still loved one another was all we ever wanted from The Beatles. John's death, the senseless infighting and so many other things seemed to rob us of that, but "Real Love" gave it back.

For being the last great Beatles record. For bringing John Lennon back to life...even if it was only for 3:56...and, for re-positioning the 'myth', "Real Love" is The Beatles 9th Most Memorable Moment.

#8 - YESTERDAY

When Paul McCartney was in that state of twilight sleep and heard a melody in his head to which he would later write some provisional lyrics...."Scrambled eggs. Oh, baby, how I love your legs"...(Little did we know that McCartney was a leg man.)...he couldn't possibly have had any idea about the impact of the song he was starting to write.

It was a great tune, of course, so instantly familiar, even to McCartney himself, that he played it for friends asking them to help him figure out who he stole it from.

It was all his own, of course. One more gorgeous ballad, the likes of which he's already started to write ("And I Love Her"). And it wouldn't have been unthinkable for he and The Beatles to record it the same way. Acoustic, yeah, but with everyone in the band playing on it. But this may have been the pivotal moment when George Martin brought his knowledge, his experience...maybe even his own musical taste to The Beatles.

First, Martin thought there'd be no place for Ringo on the song. (Well, there would have been had he been inclined to find one... maracas, using just his brushes.) During rehearsals, the band tried a variety of ways to work the song up...including doing it with an organ before Sir George persuaded the others to let Paul record it alone. Then...the big step. He suggested that he write a string arrangement for the song. Strings? On a Beatles' record?? Well, he won the moment... and contemporary music changed forever because he did. (And, there had been strings on lots and lots of rock records before this. And, by rockers, I mean. Not wanna be crooners. The Everlys used them on "Let It Be Me". Fats Domino used them on "Walkin' To New Orleans". But, with "Yesterday", they were much more nuanced. They had a true classical feel to them...part of the reason why I said what I did about Martin bringing his own tastes into the group's music.)

It changed things in two ways...immediately. First, The Beatles, from the start of their time at EMI, were a four man band...with rare exceptions (Andy White on "Love Me Do" and "PS I Love You" being one instance, George Martin's invaluable keyboard work being the other.)

With "Yesterday", The Beatles...in this case...became a one man band. It was the first track the band recorded...after 9 singles, four albums and an EP...that didn't include all the members of the band. This broke down one wall. From this point on, everybody didn't have to be on every track. Whatever combination of the band that made a song work best... even if it was only one of them...could be used in its realization.

More than that, it meant that a "Beatles track' could be any track that any of them appeared on which they deemed appropriate of the title (which is why "Yesterday" is a Beatles' track...and "I'm The Greatest"... which has three times as many Beatles on it...isn't.)

With the string section added to it, that also meant that Beatles music was no more limited to the instruments that the group themselves and George Martin could play. (That wall really came down four months earlier when Martin brought in Johnnie Scott to play flute on "You've Got To Hide Your Love Away"...and I would love to know how Sir George talked John Lennon...whose song it was, obviously...into that.) That opened the door to the violins and horns...and tambouras and tablas we would hear in Beatles music from then on.

And the reverberations of that...like everything The Beatles did... was felt throughout rock and roll's creative community.

Within a year, the horizon had been broadened for the whole genre...virtually everybody was putting string and brass on their records. Simon & Garfunkel with "The Dangling Conversation", Dylan with "Rainy Day Women #12 & 35", even the Stones with their regrettable copy of "Yesterday"..."As Tears Go By".

And, of course, more than the instruments that were being used, the fact that artists were no longer limited to guitars, keyboards, a sax and drums opened the door to everyone beginning to experiment with what kinds of songs they could write. The Beatles, of course, taking it further and doing it better than anyone else.

And, with that, the walls came tumblin' down. Rock and roll would soon include influences not just from gospel and country, but from virtually all forms of music. And that would transform rock into the most vital, most creative style of music the world would ever hear.

Beyond that, "Yesterday" was the first obvious standard to come from The Beatles. With it, the members of the music establishment had to begin giving The Beatles some grudging respect, no longer being able to say that their earlier great songs were creative accidents.

It became the most recorded song of all time...perhaps, rightfully so, as well.

But, because it so redefined The Beatles work, their reputation, so broadened where their music (and everybody else's) could go. And because it showed them that it was all right to have people who weren't Beatles playing on their records...and all right not to have people who were Beatles not playing on them, too...and what that would ultimately mean to the group's tomorrows..."Yesterday" was The Beatles 8th Most Memorable Moment.

#7 - THE MURDER OF JOHN LENNON

I don't know where you were when you heard about it. I was driving home from a part time job I had. It was about 9 o'clock Pacific time. I couldn't believe it. John Lennon was dead...killed by some deranged fan. I was up all night, taking phone calls from friends...from people I hadn't heard from in years...reconnecting just to share their shock, their grief.

It seems that my story matches that of much of the world that mourned this unspeakably senseless loss of this man who spoke so eloquently to the world through his music. There were reactions, tributes and memorials seldom given to heads of state or major religious figures.

And we mourned individually, as if each of us had lost a close friend. Part of that, of course, was because of our love for Lennon...and The Beatles, but John shared so much of his life with us in his music that, though few of us would be lucky enough to meet him, a lot of us felt that not only was he a part of our lives, but that we were a part of his.

The story headlined newspapers around the country and around the world. Lennon would be on the cover of "Time", "Newsweek" and other national publications. Unprecedented for a guy who made records for a living. The coverage of his death was akin to that given to a world leader...but, in many ways, John...and all The Beatles...were that, too.

On the Sunday after his death, Yoko asked for everyone to observe ten minutes of silence in his name. Radio stations actually went quiet during that time. I mean silence. No music. No commercials. Silence out of love and respect for the man. 30,000 people gathered in Liverpool. 225,000 gathered in Central Park, not far from John and Yoko's home in the Dakota. Three fans themselves committed suicide in response to Lennon's murder.

And, of course, there would be tributes. Not long after, a memorial was built in his honor in Central Park, called, fittingly, "Strawberry Fields". Every year, on the anniversary of his death, a memorial is staged at the Capitol Records building in Hollywood. And there is even a permanent John Lennon Memorial Society in Portland, Oregon which raises money to feed those in need...answering John's call in "Imagine" that there is, in fact, no need for greed or hunger. And, naturally, Lennon...and the manner of his passing...would be remembered in music, too...by Freddie Mercury and Queen ("Life Is Real"...playing off Lennon's line from "Love", where he sang "love is real"), by Pink Floyd's David Gilmour ("Murder"), by Elton John ("Empty Garden (Hey Hey Johnnie)" and, of course by George Harrison... with Paul and Ringo...("All Those Years Ago").

But, as significant a figure as John Lennon was, the world was probably not so much grieving the loss of John Lennon, as the loss of The Beatles because when John died, The Beatles...and all they represented...died with him. And the fact that Lennon and McCartney never reconciled (publicly, at least) before John's murder.

As brilliant a singer and songwriter as he was, John Lennon was much more than that, or the world would never have reacted to his passing as it did. He combined his art with activism as no one else had previously...or since, really...done. He understood that, with great success comes great responsibility...echoing and living, oddly enough, Luke's words from his 'Parable of the Faithful Servant'..."To whomever much is given, of him will much be required". And Lennon, rarely, shirked from that self-decided responsibility. And, amazingly, did little damage to his reputation and his career in the process...none of it, obviously, permanent.

The measure of a man's life can sometimes be better measured not in what he did while he lived, but what he might have done had he not died. Paul, George and Ringo continued to give us great work for decades after John left us. Let's say that Lennon lived into his mid 70's. Even at an album every three or four years...and that's probably a pretty good guess seeing what the other guys in the band did...That would have been another 12 albums worth of John's music. Easily more than 100 songs that John is now singing to the angels.

And one can certainly assume that, if, after 25 years of growing up, Paul, George and Ringo chose to work together that John would have been there, too...and "Real Love" might, in fact, have been an actual reunion recording. (And Lennon might have been the one to champion the idea. May Pang disclosed on "The Beatles Show" that John wanted the band to get together in the Fall of 1974 to record a new track..."and, if that works, we'll do another", he told her.)

As The Beatle...ex-Beatle...whatever...who spoke out most about world issues, world problems, you can only wonder what he would say today about things like the blunting of our civil rights, government intrusion into our private lives, the demonizing of minorities of all kinds and, certainly, commerce driven wars, like our frivolous, unjustifiable massacre in Iraq.

John was the 'tough guy' in The Beatles. Listen to his lyrics on songs like "You Can't Do That" and "Run For Your Life" (where he virtually threatens to 'off' his girlfriend). Hear how he pushes us around vocally... telling us often to "look out" or "watch out". Yet, he'd be the guy who'd craft The Beatles' worldwide message of unity "All You Need Is Love."

Like almost all of us, John lived within his contradictions. He could be sarcastic...cruel, even. He could be crazy, witty, insightful, charming, ego-maniacal. The difference between him and the rest of the world was he was doing it with a million spotlights on him and with everybody watching...And he was never afraid to let us see who he really was.
I don't know too many other people who were as strong and as brave as that.

There is, as I've said and, hopefully, by this point, shown the amazing amount of irony in The Beatles' story, but this is the most tragic example of this...by far. This guy who would ultimately be seen as a man of peace would lose his far too short a life in a ridiculously senseless act of gun violence...as if there is any other kind.

One person described him this way..."He was a warm man who cared a lot and with..."Give Peace A Chance" helped stop the Vietnam War". The person describing John was Paul McCartney who probably knew him better, longer than anyone on earth.

Because of the effect his death had on The Beatles, the world of music and the world in general, the death of John Lennon is The Beatles 7th most memorable moment.

#6 - RINGO JOINS THE BEATLES

Richard Starkey was a sickly youngster, who became obsessed with rock and roll and playing the drums. He became a local celebrity and an acknowledged musician long before he joined The Beatles when he was part of Rory Storm & the Hurricanes.

He met the band while they were all in Germany...Ringo still being the drummer for the Hurricanes. Back in England, occasionally, he would play with John, Paul & George, filling in for Pete Best. And it was clear then that, no matter how great The Beatles sounded. No matter how successful Starr was without them, they would both be better off working together.

So, what did Ringo Starr bring to The Beatles? Well, there are a number of 'compare and contrast' examples...songs that The Beatles recorded with Pete Best on drums that they also recorded with Ringo on drums. If you play those duplicate songs back to back, there could be no debate over who was the better drummer. Beyond his own talent, George Harrison would say, decades later, that the band just seemed to 'jell' with Ringo as drummer. And Harrison was the one who, in fact, campaigned to have Ringo replace Pete Best in The Beatles.

And Ringo's own growth as a musician, maybe exemplified better than anyone else that of the entire group. He was a great rock drummer...that sheet of white noise coming nonstop from his cymbals was a perfect foundation for the high energy music that came from the band early on.

Then, as the band matured, he became perhaps the most creative, most intelligent drummer in rock history. Never the fastest, never the flashiest. But the one man who mastered the technique of using his brains when playing an instrument dominated by brawn.

Coming up with some of the most innovative drum patterns, always the most appropriate drum fills. And, beyond that, the fact that Ringo played left handed gave his drumming a most unique sound. Because he would lead with his left hand rather than his right, his fills always sounded like they were being played backwards...or inside out. Anyway, his singular style behind the kit was a defining musical style point with The Beatles. You hear the drums played that way, sound that way, you always know it's Ringo. Few drummers develop that sort of groove.

Besides that and beyond the music, Ringo seemed to fit in with John, Paul, and George personally better than the more withdrawn Best. That probably was vital during the best/worst days of Beatlemania when the group would, often, spend 30 minutes on stage and the other 23 1/2 hours a day locked in a hotel.

When The Beatles hit in America, it was Ringo who was, probably, the best known and best loved Beatle. Ringo was so likable and so non-threatening that, he, maybe by himself, won over America's parents to the band.

And even after the mania subsided, he was the 'everyman' in the group. Everybody could relate to him...and, therefore, The Beatles...no matter how long the hair and the beards got. No matter how far out the music sounded. No matter how many nude album covers or drug busts came from the others, Ringo was still there and that meant that The Beatles were still The Beatles.

He was called the luckiest guy in show business, a hanger-on with drumsticks. (Lorne Michaels even joked that John, Paul and George could give him a lesser split of the $3000 he offered the band to reunite on "Saturday Night Live".) All because he worked with such other obviously talented men. Well, as his solo career proved, knocking Ringo's own genius because of the other geniuses he worked with is like calling a guy whose 6'11" 'short' because he hangs around with guys who are 7'1".

Maybe his greatest contribution is the fact that the rest of the group loved him as much as we did. His ability to get along with John, Paul & George after the break up. They all wrote for him, played and sang with him...as we said, on the "Ringo" album and long before and after, too. It is clear that he kept the lines of communication open between the four of them during the tough last days of the group...and the even tougher days that came after (as is proven that he was the one chosen to work things out with McCartney over holding back Paul's first solo LP).

Later he would become an actor, singer and songwriter of note. Yes, all due to the fact that he was a Beatle, but your résumé only carries you so far if you can't do the work...And Ringo's work has been excellent for more than 50 years.

And he kept The Beatles' sermon of peace and love alive by preaching it longer and, maybe better any other Beatle. (And none of them believed it more passionately than he did).

For his becoming the fourth side of the circle, Ringo Starr joining The Beatles is the group's 6th Most Memorable Moment.

#5 - GEORGE HARRISON JOINS THE BEATLES

How many friendships have you had that have lasted half a century? Well, first you'd have to be 50 years old to answer that question, but my guess is very few...and all of them extremely important, extremely close.

The span of their friendship...from before Harrison turned 14 until McCartney was nearly 60...45 years...showed just how long The Beatles were a part of each other's lives...and of ours. In fact, Paul knew George before he knew John Lennon.

It was a chance meeting on a bus when, on their way to school, two students...Paul McCartney and George Harrison happened to sit together and began discussing a shared passion...rock and roll. I can't imagine another school bus conversation that would so change the lives of the people having it...and, in the course of that, also change the world.

But Harrison wasn't just obsessed about Elvis, Little Richard and Buddy Holly on the way to school, he was so preoccupied by the subject that his attention would drift away from what his teachers were saying once he was in class and he would spend his time instead drawing pictures of guitars.

It all started when he heard...who else?...Elvis Presley singing..."what else?..."Heartbreak Hotel" as he passed a neighbor's house. Game, set and match. His father would buy him a $10 guitar. A family friend would teach him chords. Once he and Paul met, they would get together after school and play...music, I mean. His precocious skills impressed McCartney, who was already in the Quarrymen, enough that he championed him to John Lennon.

The two would meet on February 6th, 1958. Lennon was unsure about adding him to his musical group. Here he was, a 17 year old man of the world and McCartney was asking him to bring a 14 year old kid into the band. And, Harrison not only was just 14, he looked it. He auditioned once. Failed. Still hung around with the band. Wound up filling in a few times. That earned him a second audition. This one on the famous 'double decker' bus.

McCartney...taking the side of the guy he wanted in the band, rather than the guy who put him in the band...urged George to play for Lennon, and Harrison went into a version of "Raunchy" (the Bill Justis instrumental that ironically...again...we would hear Paul, George and Ringo play on the bonus DVD of "The Beatles Anthology"). Lennon must have been very impressed because, young or not, he realized that Harrison had become too good a musician for John to keep him out of his band.

And, at that point, The Beatles were 3/4 of the way home.

And the three of them had to deal with the frustration, the depression, the anger that must have come with the continual rejection, discounting and condescension that comes when you're looking for success harder than success is looking for you.

But, what would have happened if Paul and George hadn't sat together, if George had taken his bike to school, if Paul went to a different school entirely?

Well, for one thing, they probably never would have become The Beatles. I mean, the Quarrymen were already together when McCartney met Harrison, but they probably wouldn't have stayed together long enough to change their name to The Beatles. For a while, in 1959, the band unofficially broke up. Then, in August of that year, it would be George who would bring The Beatles...or the Quarrymen at that point...back together. The Les Stewart Quartet was supposed to play at the Kasbah Club...Yes, the one owned by Pete Best's mom, Mona, but they got into an argument and cancelled the gig. Harrison heard about it told John and Paul and the Quarrymen wound up playing the gig instead...So The Beatles both started...and ended their career because of four guys in a band who couldn't get along with one another. Different bands, though.

Without George Harrison, The Beatles wouldn't have had a lead guitarist...Well, they would have had one...probably Paul...but they wouldn't have had one who, within just a few years, would become (with James Burton) probably the master rock music lead guitarist, being able to play a symphony with two hands...and do it in 12 measures...defining the idiom of what a great instrumental break should sound like in a 3 minute rock record. Tuneful. Creative. Efficient. Memorable. Beautiful. And no one has come along since to do it better.

And they wouldn't have had a lead guitarist who made it sound like he was playing a six string carillon. That incredibly melodic sound that came from Harrison's guitar is still one of my favorite trademarks of the group.

They wouldn't have had a third great lead singer...underrated as he was...far more within the band and by George Martin than he was by any of us. They couldn't have been 50% better than the Everly Brothers at singing harmonies without George adding his voice to John and Paul's. And those three guys together gave us some of the richest, most gorgeous vocal work ever to be heard...ever.

If George Harrison had never met Paul, Eastern music would never have found its way into Western culture. Eastern culture probably would never have found its way here, either.

Yeah, Harrison said The Beatles invented Jimi Hendrix and MTV, but George Harrison probably invented the Community College meditation class and every Indian restaurant that exists on these shores.

Without Harrison meeting Paul, there would be no Christian rock. Religious music had been around since the time of Jesus. And those songs got turned into hits as soon as they learned to put grooves in shellac. Mostly, they were spirituals or traditional hymns...the Orioles original of "Crying In The Chapel", Laurie London's "He's Got The Whole World In His Hand" (produced by George Martin, as we mentioned earlier). Harrison, beginning with "The Inner Light" and "Long Long Long", made a cottage industry of the writing of new songs of praise. Yeah, no George Harrison, no Amy Grant or Stryper, no Dove Awards or religious pop radio formats.

If Harrison hadn't gotten into The Beatles, he wouldn't have been able to have gotten out of them. He started his own band before he joined John and Paul (a three man group called the Rebels) and played, for a time, with another band while things were dry for the Quarrymen, so he might have pursued a career in music. But, as talented as he was, how far would he have gone. ('Guitar groups were dead', remember?

Until The Beatles became rock and roll's version of the defibrillator.)

If contemporary music would have continued to be a sea of Paul and Paula, Freddie Cannon and Little Joey and the Fips ("Bongo Stomp"... actually a top 30 in 1962), seems that there wouldn't have been much taste for the music George would have been making. He probably would never have made it in Britain, much less America and, other than playing weekends to pick up some extra cash, probably would have wound up in the job he was beginning to train for before music became his life... and vice versa. Electrician.

Without Paul and George hooking up, no Beatles, no post-Beatles for George. So, no "All Things Must Pass", no "33 1/3", no "Cloud Nine", no "Brainwashed" and all the other marvelous work he gave us spread out over four decades with, no doubt, more to come.

No Wilburys, the superest of all supergroups.

No Bangladesh...and probably none of the great rock charity events that came after. (Hard to think that 22,000 people would fill Madison Square Garden...twice...to see Chubby Checker and Johnny Crawford, regardless of the cause.)

All because of a bus ride.

Maybe you should pay attention to whom your kids are sitting next to on the school bus. Your kid may be the next George Harrison and the other kid could be the next Paul McCartney.

George Harrison joining The Beatles. The group's 5th Most Memorable Moment.

#4 - JOHN LENNON MEETS PAUL McCARTNEY

I don't know what 15 year old Paul McCartney was expecting to find when he went to St. Peter's Church for the Woolton Town Fete...a local celebration...but what he wound up finding was immortality.

He was there in the late afternoon and, as he arrived, a skiffle band was on stage playing and singing. The band was known as the Quarrymen and their leader was John Lennon...who, even then, couldn't remember the lyrics to the songs he was singing. (He apparently made up lyrics to songs like "Come Go With Me", scatting as he sang them...which caught Paul's ear). And, if Lennon still had work to do memorizing his lines, so to speak, he already had his on-stage swagger down pat. That caught McCartney's eye. So, Lennon had an instant fan in this 15 year old from Allerton.

During a half hour break in between sets, McCartney went over, introduced himself and, no doubt, the two started talking music. McCartney grabbed a guitar and began playing the Eddie Cochran song "Twenty Flight Rock". Paul knew all the words to the song. John and the rest of the group were amazed. "Nobody knew all the words to "Twenty Flight Rock", the Quarrymen thought, "maybe not even Eddie Cochran". And, McCartney had an instant fan in Lennon.

After the meeting, Lennon had a hard decision to make...Does he let someone as talented as Paul into the band to make it better, knowing that would mean he might not be the sole focus of attention any longer? Well, he made the right decision, offered Paul a spot in the band and on somewhere around the 23rd day of July, 1957, John Lennon and Paul McCartney became friends, partners, collaborators...and, eventually, co-legends.

Lennon and McCartney, as high school students, worked almost obsessively to become better guitarists, better singers and, ultimately, better songwriters. Both supporting and competing with one another as to who could write the better song...that 'tug of war' that produced the greatest catalog of contemporary music ever to come from two men writing together.

Unfortunately, it continued, in a different form after the group split up. Reportedly, John was jealous of Paul's burgeoning solo success and, supposedly, McCartney was rankled that Lennon's solo music was seen as having all the gravitas while he was seen as nothing more than a lightweight. But, by then, they were no longer working with one another so that each couldn't fill in the other's gaps. In fact, during the first years after the break up, they probably weren't even speaking to one another.

And, yeah, it would be the most classic case of not realizing how great something was until it wasn't any longer. I think we all understood that...John and Paul, too, after a time, I would bet. Lapses in judgment that each made alone, that the other would never have let happen had they still been together. Had the partnership endured, there would have been no 'Woman Is The...Of The World' from John, no "Mumbo" from Paul...and that's just one example from each. There are certainly others.

And, though John was the one who announced he was walking away from the band, I've always thought that Paul was the fulcrum to having The Beatles reunite.

He was the one who kept them together after Brian's death. He would be the one who pushed them apart. When Lennon wanted the reunion in '74, Paul was too busy and, probably, too successful to consider it. When Paul wanted the reunion, Lennon was dead. But he worked as hard to bring The Beatles back together in the 90's as he did to keep them together in the 60's. We'll probably never know this until all parties are gone, but I'm sure that Paul went to extreme lengths... making sacrifices that had to be very difficult for him (Jeff Lynne over George Martin to produce the reunion sessions???) just to placate everyone...to get the thing going and keep it going.

And everything we've gotten since The Beatles began working together as the executive producers of their legacy is probably because of Paul's decisions to make them happen.

John may have been labeled as the leader, but someone said...and I don't remember who...but someone who would know...that that was only because Lennon was the guy who spoke first. Another insider said that, from early on, The Beatles were really Paul's band with McCartney working the egos and the angles quietly from the inside to get done what he felt was best for the group.

He became the voice of The Beatles...singing lead on their most important latter day singles. And, to much of the world, the face of The Beatles, too. 'Sgt. Pepper' was his. So was "Abbey Road". For better or worse, so were the "Get Back" sessions. But, as The Beatles got to the top of one creative mountain, it would be Paul who'd put another mountain in front of them and lead the rest of the band to the top of it.

But the fact that there were no more 'Pepper's or "Abbey Road's or "Hey Jude's to come from McCartney once on his own tells you how much The Beatles gave to him.

To me, the saddest thing about the end of The Beatles...other than the four of them never having a real reunion in the studio...was that John and Paul never, it seemed, really reconciled. (Paul admitted seeing a therapist after Lennon's murder to talk about their relationship...That doesn't happen if you're best friends again.)

I don't know if you've ever had a very close relationship that fractured. I have. Even if there are apologies and amends on both sides, it's just never the same. And, I bet that's how it was with John and Paul. No matter how much time they spent together after The Beatles broke up, no matter how enjoyable it was, there was probably a distance between them that nothing could narrow. A heart break.

Even now, you have to wonder which feeling within McCartney is stronger...the joy of John asking him to join the band and everything that came after...or the regret over his part in how they fell apart and, for decades, stayed apart.

Paul McCartney joining The Beatles...The group's 4th Most Memorable Moment.

#3 - JOHN LENNON STARTS 'THE BLACK JACKS'

Like a lot of teenagers in the mid 50's, John Lennon was looking for direction.

And he unwittingly found it when he first heard Elvis Presley (once more..."Heartbreak Hotel"). (If The Beatles invented MTV, Jimi Hendrix, Christian rock, the music video and the charity concert, it looks like "Heartbreak Hotel" invented The Beatles.)

Up until then, John had little contact with popular music. The family rarely had the radio on...unlike what happened in the McCartney and Harrison households. He was mostly raised on country music (which can explain his instant affinity to people like Presley and Buddy Holly). But once Lennon heard about that place at the end of Lonely Street where lovers go to cry away their gloom, rock and roll became 'the only thing that got through to him', as he would later say. "That was life" to quote him.

Much has been written about the wild life of John's mother, Julia. How she left John to stay with her sister, Lennon's beloved 'Aunt Mimi'. But she and her son would see each other often...almost every day, in fact, as he became a teenager. While Mimi tried to discourage John's love of music, it was Julia who taught John chords on the banjo, would host rehearsals for the Quarrymen at her home and would buy Lennon his first guitar. Apparently, it cost half of what the cheap instrument that George's father got his son did. (That's what prompted McCartney's remark in "The Beatles Anthology" about it being "guaranteed not crack". I would guess that Les Paul never shopped for a guitar on the basis of its unbreakability.)

One of the first songs he ever learned to play was Fats Domino's "Ain't That A Shame".
Then came "That'll Be The Day". Then, "Johnny B. Goode" and "Carol".

He soon formed a band with a school mate...Pete Shotton.. For a week, the band was called the Black Jacks. Soon, and for a long time thereafter, they would be called the Quarrymen...after John's high school.

Then Paul joined the group. Then George. Along with nearly a dozen other people along the way, many of whom left, no doubt, because they didn't want to waste any more time with a band that seemed to be headed nowhere...man.

They would play at a party for people who worked at a slaughter house, church socials, weddings. (They played at the reception where George's brother, Harry and his wife got married...and they played for free. That was at the end of 1959. A year and a half into things and The Beatles, at times, still had to work for nothing.) (By the way, the Quarrymen reformed...playing skiffle and early rock and roll...in 1994... with five of the original members of the band...and continues to work today as we write this.)

Then Stuart Sutcliffe would join the band (January of 1960). In August, they would head for Germany and were obligated to have a drummer, so Pete Best was brought in.

In Hamburg, they found their chops, their confidence and presence and their act.

They came home, conquered Liverpool, then the north of England. Booted Pete Best, brought in Ringo and the band...already matchless at this point...became absolutely 'sans pareil'.

EMI said "yes" where Decca said, "no". They would then take London, all of England, America and the whole world within 18 months. (I just read where it took Pepsi that long to make a single commercial. Honestly.)

Lennon was, at once, both a pillar of strength and a lightning rod for The Beatles.

He was not their leader (as we just said, though they may not have even known it, Paul was). It seemed like Lennon was their spokesman... always with a quip or a quote. And he would be the one who'd occasionally risk being impolite...to put it mildly.

He was the most outspoken, the most brash, the most controversial, and, yet, the most vulnerable. That bravado that McCartney saw on the stage at St. Peter's was not an act, but a part of his internal design. Psychologists would call that one of his 'ego defenses'. John trying to mask the childhood pain (and we are all still children) of being rejected by both of his parents and the fear of being rejected by everyone else.

He wrote the most adventurous lyrics in the band. The wittiest. The most political and the most personal. From early on, listening to the structure of some of his first songs, it was clear that he was hearing music in a way almost nobody else did.

Honestly, though Paul had the grand ideas for the band...it was John who really made those ideas grand. 'Sgt. Pepper' would have been not much more than a collection of dandy pop songs without "Lucy In The Sky With Diamonds", Being For The Benefit Of Mr. Kite" and, of course, "A Day In The Life". (And who knows how much McCartney was influenced to push his own musical boundaries on that album by working with Lennon.)

It was Lennon who gave the initial direction to the group's most groundbreaking music...bringing "Tomorrow Never Knows" into the studio as the first song the band would work on for "Revolver" and "Strawberry Fields Forever" as the first song for 'Pepper'. Whereas McCartney expanded the limits as to the styles of music one could find coming from a rock band, Lennon expanded the limits of the sounds themselves.

Because of Paul, the Beatles were hit makers. Because of John, they were groundbreakers. The Beatles iconic legend rests virtually with John Lennon.

And because of that amazing non-stop symphony going on in his head, Lennon was probably most responsible among The Beatles for turning the recording studio into a place where music was created rather than where a live performance was replicated.

His talents as a singer were an homage to Elvis. Lennon was a white man who could sing black. He was probably one of the best in the little discussed role of rhythm guitarist...what he played would fill out the arrangements in The Beatles music, rather than just add another instrument to it.

He was the first man to come in to The Beatles and the first one to go out of them. He would work hard to establish his own individual name in music and, then, he would leave it all when the chance came for him to be a father. He would become pop music's...and, maybe, pop culture's first real activist, never being afraid to take a stand on an issue in spite of...and, as some might say, because of what it might do to him or his career. (And self destructiveness was, indeed also a part of his makeup.)

He became pop culture's first martyr, which produced decades' worth of accolades Lennon himself probably would have laughed at.

But, for all of his contributions, ultimately, John Lennon will be remembered for deciding to form a garage band. "Mostly", he would say, "we just played for fun". Yes, John, it's been that...and so much more...for 50 years...going on eternity.

John Lennon forming the Black Jacks. The Beatles 3rd Most Memorable Moment.

#2 - SGT. PEPPER

When do you think they began to see it?...The Beatles, I mean. When do you think they began to have some understanding that what they were working on was more than just their next step ahead, but something that was a thousand miles from where they'd already taken contemporary music? "Sgt. Pepper's Lonely Hearts Club Band".

They could look back and see it, from the beginning, just like we did. The Beatles' growth as songwriters. The big leap forward that came with "Help!" where the days of strictly boy/girl relationship songs were over and where the boundaries began being expanded...their own and those of the music itself as to what could be said in a rock record and how, lyrically and musically, it could be expressed. "Rubber Soul" showed unmistakably that the group was growing up as singers, composers, musicians. The lyrics were far more sophisticated, more witty and wise than anything we'd gotten before...not just from The Beatles but from anybody in rock and roll...and the door was opening. It got knocked down completely with "Revolver" the album that expanded the boundaries of rock and roll to include sounds and styles of music that fans of the genre not only never heard in a rock record, but probably never heard at all. All of a sudden, the Top 40 became a lesson in world music.

By the time they got to 'Pepper', though, they had gone beyond challenging the conventions of the songs that filled their albums to challenging the conventions of albums themselves. Only, with 'Pepper', they didn't challenge them as much as do away with them completely; in every way. The traditional three second 'rill' between songs was gone, replaced by cross-fades, reprises, sudden stops, songs coming in where they'd fit musically...on a particular beat...to give the sense of one continual piece of music.

The record lasted more than 37 minutes...nearly filling up both sides of vinyl. Some albums from other artists were lasting a bit more than half that. (Check your DC5 albums. It will probably take you longer to find one of them than to play it. Their "Satisfied With You" LP clocks in at about 20 minutes.) (And American Beatle albums weren't all that much better..."Something New" comes in at under 25.)

The songs themselves lasted longer, too. The Beatles had expanded seemingly every other aspect of their music by the time they got to the Summer of Love. The one boundary that was left was time. Up to then, the longest track from The Beatles was "You Really Got A Hold On Me" (3:02). Two songs on 'Sgt. Pepper' (Within You, Without You" and "A Day In The Life") went more than five...That's a 60 % increase in the size of their musical canvas...and, in both cases, The Beatles made the most of it. (By the way, this was crossing a dangerous barrier. Stations didn't play records that lasted more than 3 minutes. It got in the way of the 18 minutes of commercials they were going to play that hour. (It got to the point where Columbia Records issued Simon & Garfunkel's "Fakin' It" with the label listing the time as '2:74'...to make the program directors...ones who weren't that good at telling time, anyway, think that the record still came in under 3 minutes.) This could have cost the band airplay which could have sabotaged its success. But, these were The Beatles and, more significantly, this was 'Sgt. Pepper'.

It all started on November 24th, 1966. The band had decided to start work on a new album and they met at Abbey Road. They hadn't seen each other since the end of August and, yet, when all four of them arrived, they had each grown facial hair...unaware that the others had done so. Maybe that was a sign of the like-mindedness that would make this album so epic.

First, they worked on "Strawberry Fields Forever". That song alone had to tell everyone involved that the band would be picking up where they left off with "Revolver" and progressing from there. Then came "When I'm 64". Then "Penny Lane"

EMI came calling early in the year for a new single from the band and 'Strawberry Fields' and "Penny Lane" wound up being it. (One of George Martin's greatest regrets from his days with The Beatles was his not including those two songs on 'Pepper'. I still wonder where he would have put them in the context of the album.)

Then came "Sgt. Pepper's Lonely Hearts Club Band", so the album had its theme...in more ways than one...and "A Day In The Life"...and the album had its north star.

After finishing that song, the band had to know that this project wasn't going to wind up being another "Beatles VI". And on it went from there.

For this album more than any other, the group continually looked for new ways to produce different sounds in the studio, constantly trying to, as one frustrated EMI engineer said years later, 'make a guitar sound like a piano and a piano sound like a guitar'. The lyrics on many of the songs were idiosyncratic...coming from circus posters ('Mr. Kite"), headlines ("A Day In The Life") and who knows where ('Lucy In the Sky'). We had heard The Beatles headed in this direction with "Rain" & "Tomorrow Never Knows"...but those were exceptions. Lyrical unconventionality was to be heard virtually everywhere. It was as if The Beatles were saying "To hell with what popular music has written about for the last 70 years. We want to write songs about anything".

The subject matter of the songs and the words used in them may have been the most obvious sign of what a departure this album really was.

Of course, the production of the album would rival that. It is one thing to have sitars and dilrubas on a song like "Within You, Without You". It's quite another to put eastern instruments on Western songs. Granted The Beatles made that breakthrough with "Norwegian Wood", but, for years and years, when I'd hear "Getting Better", I wondered how The Beatles put a buzz saw on that track (and, I guess, who tuned it). That whole side of the affair you can credit to George Martin (and Geoff Emerick, the album's engineer). The Beatles came to him with ideas...however vague...about how they wanted things to sound and... with 1967 electronics...well, you heard how it came out. He pushed the limits of what today would be charitably called primitive studio equipment...George Martin being able to coax a level of innovation out of four track tape machines that probably couldn't be done today in the limitless world of digital recording.

But The Beatles wouldn't stop at revolutionizing the tunes they wrote...or the words they wrote for them...or even how they sounded as they were being recorded. Even the packaging was groundbreaking... bold, loud and, yes, psychedelic. A full gatefold album jacket...a first for a single disc set. And inserts of cut outs so that, you too, could become a member of Sgt. Pepper's band. Even a specially designed paper sleeve for the record.

Beyond that, they offered a libretto...the lyrics printed on the back cover...implying that the words to the songs were important enough, or, at least, interesting enough to be read. Credits on the record jacket...well deserved...for Martin and Emerick. Another first.

The cover itself was a collection of The Beatles' heroes done by Peter Blake. And it was as eclectic a collection of people as the album was an eclectic collection of songs. Marilyn Monroe was there. So was George Bernard Shaw, Lawrence of Arabia, WC Fields and Sonny Liston. Jesus Christ, Adolph Hitler and Mahatma Gandhi were supposed to be among them, but were not included to avoid controversy. Leo Gorcey (from the Bowery Boys) was supposed to be included...but he wanted $400 to give his permission. (If anyone should have gotten the checkbook out, it was Gorcey...who wasn't exactly the busiest actor in Hollywood by 1967.) The Beatles were there twice...as Sgt. Pepper's band and, in wax, as the moptops. And not only were John, Paul, George and Ringo part of the cover, so was Stuart Sutcliffe and, also, you find medals that came from the family of Pete Best. So, the six men most readily called 'Beatles' were all represented. (And, of course, the cover remains one of the most iconic of all record sleeves. Imitated dozens of times for albums from other artists.)

After the end of the world piano crash from "A Day In The Life", they included a tone that could only be heard by dogs...so minute was their attention to detail. And after that, three seconds or so of gibberish added to the inner groove of the record that would loop...meaning, in a sense, that 'Sgt. Pepper' would never end.

As many people have said, 'Sgt. Pepper' was neither the group's best album, nor their best work as songwriters. They're probably right. But the whole record was trippy, off center...in a variety of ways...as to how the songs were written, recorded, performed or produced...and it varied in degree from track to track, but it was there.

Moreover, it was a beat group giving us something extremely off beat...an absolutely unorthodox co-mingling of two widely divergent styles of music...and of thought...the mid-Victorian and the psychedelic. (To give you a visual, imagine wearing a morning coat and an ascot tie along with tie-dyed jeans...with holes in them.) it was the super-conservative and the extremely liberal somehow going back and forth that created some new quirky hybrid that even The Beatles probably didn't intend and that's what gave an unmistakable unity to the entire album start to finish...in spite of what John Lennon would often say to the contrary.

It was recorded over five months, nearly 50 sessions taking more than 535 hours of studio time. And this from the band that recorded its first album pretty much in 535 minutes. The production costs were the equivalent of nearly half a million dollars in today's money. (Still a worthwhile investment, wouldn't you say?) And it threw down the gauntlet to the rest of rock music's elite. Everyone from the Stones ("Their (unfortunate) Satanic Majesties Request' (Stick to what you do best, guys...stealing old blues riffs.), to the Who ("Tommy", "Quadrophenia") to the Mothers Of Invention ("We're Only In It For The Money" (which parroted both the album and its cover) to the Four Seasons ("The Genuine Imitation Life Gazette") and on tried to outdo 'Pepper' and, of course, they wound up all being done in by it.

It led to a number of covers of the entire album. What a tribute to it! And those tributes were not limited to music. There was an off-Broadway stage show..."Sgt. Pepper's Lonely Hearts Club Band On The Road". That led to the film that was named after the album. The Bee Gees and Peter Frampton as place markers for The Beatles. According to critics, the movie was like "Magical Mystery Tour" only done by someone other than John, Paul, George and Ringo. It barely broke even, but, how many other movies were inspired by a rock and roll album? (Apple Corps is listed as one of the studios that produced the film, by the way...Probably just part of the deal to license the songs and the name. Most likely, there was no involvement by The Beatles' company in the actual making of the film...At least, I hope not.) The soundtrack album from the film would be produced by George Martin which meant that the music coming from it would be as good as it could be without The Beatles performing it. And the three hits to come from it (Aerosmith's version of "Come Together", Robin Gibb doing "Oh! Darling" and Earth Wind and Fire's million selling cover of "Got To Get You Into My Life") were outstanding. (The double LP would go multiplatinum...and that's what put the film in the black.)

The album itself would be re-done an amazing number of times in an amazing number of different styles over the decades. There have been plenty of tribute albums done for certain artists, but 'Pepper' was, probably, the first case of tribute albums being done for an album. And Cheap Trick has taken the album on the road and done it live...start to finish.

To say any more about the impact of the album would only be stating the obvious, but, to show you how lasting that impact is, in 2005...nearly 40 years after its release, Rolling Stone still named 'Sgt. Pepper' as the 'greatest album of all time'. And, even if that wasn't the case, it is probably the most influential album of all time.

It was the first rock album to win the "Album of the Year" Grammy...at a time when the record industry was still dominated by crooners and people who worked in and with big bands. Guys who hated rock and roll because the music and the people making it weren't as intelligent, weren't as sophisticated and weren't as talented as they were...yet, they were selling all the records. (That's why the recording industry started NARAS in 1957...no coincidence about the date. Rock and roll had arrived and the Grammys were a clear message as to what songs, albums and artists the music establishment thought was worthy of honoring.) Winning the award, though, was a major statement...not just for The Beatles, but for the entire genre. It legitimatized rock and roll which was, from that time forward, respected for its artistry and its innovation.

Regardless of whether it was great, greater or greatest, regardless of how well it sold...and estimates now have the album at 35 million copies...what it did to change the perception of rock and roll...to every generation in the music business and out of it...may be its greatest legacy.

But 'Pepper's' influence may have stretched into another, little considered area. Some psychologist might say that, with that, The Beatles unconsciously realized they had no place else to go as a band, so they started to go their separate ways. And, in another weird twist in The Beatles' story, 'Sgt. Pepper' might not only have taken The Beatles to the top of the mountain, it may have, ultimately, pushed them off of it.

The Beatles would do wonderful, classic, groundbreaking albums before this and after but they would never be so completely, constantly, and obsessively innovative for 40 minutes at one time than they were with 'Sgt. Pepper'.

For decades upon decades of great achievements together and apart, for The Beatles, there was none greater than "Sgt. Pepper's Lonely Hearts Club Band". The Beatles 2nd Most Memorable Moment.

#1 - ED SULLIVAN

There are only a handful of events that the people I've met in the course of my life can say that they knew exactly where they were when they happened.

The attack on Pearl Harbor, the assassination of JFK, man landing on the moon, 9/11, and The Beatles' appearance on Ed Sullivan. Four events that changed the course of American, even human history...and a pop band appearing on a variety show.

But, of course, The Beatles playing Sullivan was more than that. It was a moment that signaled what would be a generations-long change among young people in this country...and perhaps, around the world. I've mentioned this before here. You only need to look in a tome called "The Billboard Book Of #1 Hits'. On page 142, you see a picture of Bobby Vinton...short, wiry hair combed up, wearing a tuxedo as you read the story of his #1, "There I've Said It Again"...a cover of a song originally a hit by Vaughn Monroe...You can head to Google to find out who he was.

On page 143, was the story of the record that succeeded it at the top spot, "I Want To Hold Your Hand". There were The Beatles. Unconventional hair...over the tops of the ears, believe it or not. Unconventional dress...collarless jackets. As we would soon hear, unconventional speech...British accents. And, as we would learn over the years, unconventional everything else.

Presley was a prototype for and a reflection of what American teenagers had been...greasy hair, combed back, jeans, the snarly look of attitude. The Beatles were a signal of...and an agent for change... intentionally or not. Hair combed down, not back...and not larded up. (Yes, the wet head was dead...Even today, I wonder why guys slick up their hair after they just shampooed it. It makes it look like they haven't washed their hair in 3 weeks.) And the way they dressed. Sorry, but Elvis looked as comfortable in a suit as Jed Clampett did. The Beatles defined upscale preppy even before there was a phrase for it. But it went way beyond the way they looked. Everything else was starting to change.

Soon, young people would begin questioning traditional attitudes... first towards music, then sex, drugs, politics, materialism, religion. The Beatles were not responsible for all of that, but they were in the middle of all of that. And Sullivan was the launching pad. Without that, they might have been one more rock band...even though a very successful one, instead of the cultural icons they still are today.

Call it happenstance, fate, God's hand, or whatever, but there had to be some reason for Ed Sullivan being at Heathrow Airport at the end of October, 1963, just as The Beatles were arriving from Sweden, so he could see the crush of thousands of young people mad to get just a glimpse of the band. Even though he had no idea who The Beatles were, that showed him that he had to find out.

Brian Epstein was somehow able to convince Sullivan to make these guys...unknown to the American audience...headliners, something Ed had never done before nor would ever do again. Epstein and the band took less money to get that guarantee, but it turned out to be the ultimate example of 'making it up on the back end'.

As they arrived in America, 'I Want To Hold Your Hand" had just hit #1...as The Beatles hoped and serendipity allowed to happen. American kids had already found out who The Beatles were and Ed Sullivan would introduce them to everybody else. Almost literally.

Upwards of 73 million people saw The Beatles' debut on Ed Sullivan. If you adjust the numbers for the growth in population, that's still the most watched regular episode of a TV series in the history of the medium. It was eight minutes when America stopped...not out of grief, not out of horror, but out of joy. The pure excitement of watching four endearing, entertaining young men play music and an audience of several hundred young people going crazy while they did it.

Certainly, the fuse was lit...with their records already climbing the charts, but The Beatles' appearance on Sullivan set off the explosion that propelled them on a year long ride. The American press and the American people glommed on to The Beatles to re-invigorate them after the death of Jack Kennedy. Everything they did, everywhere they went was news. It was like being locked in Space Mountain for a year. One twelve month, non-stop thrill ride. There was the flood of hit singles, then one album after another after another after another. Then "A Hard Day's Night". Then the American tour.

And, of course, after the Sullivan show gave them the keys to the United States, taking over the rest of the world came in short order.

And, once The Beatles hit here...and everywhere, record company executives were scrambling to sign any band wearing bangs and speaking with British accents. (And, before them, no British music act could attract attention...even if they were wearing neon.) In a real way, bands like the Stones, the Who, the Kinks, the Animals, the Yardbirds, the DC5, Cream, Jimi Hendrix, even the Clash and the Police years later owe their fame...and their fortunes...to The Beatles. And those are only the ones who made the Rock and Roll Hall of Fame.

And another thing that makes The Beatles' appearance on Ed Sullivan so unique, so essential is that it'll never happen again. Nobody will ever be as big as The Beatles were...are. And it won't even be close.

The Ed Sullivan Show was a national get together. End of the weekend. Family home. Everybody sits down just before the kids go to bed to get up for school the next morning to see who Ed had on the show this week.

In the 60's, we had only three networks, a one out of three chance, at worst, that you were going to tune in to Ed Sullivan. Most families back then had only one set. What somebody watched, everybody watched. Today, we have, what 500 channels? How many TV's do you have in your house? I've got four of them...not counting a couple of portables I can take with me...and I don't watch any of them.

Back when, you had one or two rock stations in a market...three in a major. They played everything. You could hear Sinatra, Zeppelin and Buck Owens in the same half hour...on the same station. Today, stations are niche formatted...If you don't like Alternative Rock, you probably don't know who The Neighbourhood is. If you don't like rap, you don't have a clue about Randy Thicke. If you can't stand country, Randy Houser sounds like a real estate salesman. (And, honestly, I don't know who any of those guys are, so don't feel bad.)

No radio station is trying to get as many of everybody as they can any more...Haven't for decades. Now, everybody's trying to get all of one group...one demographic. Probably 80 or 90 % of the audience would never even be exposed to The Beatles music if they were just coming on the scene today.

And there'd be no Ed Sullivan Show for everybody in America to watch them together...in their own homes. With the growth of cable... and the shrinkage in audiences watching any one thing (because there are so many other things to watch), programming budgets have been slashed. Variety shows like Ed's have gone the way of the carburetor. The Beatles would have to go on everything from "Celebrity Apprentice" to "Under The Dome" to "WWE Raw" to "the PBS News Hour" to reach just a fraction of the audience that saw them on that magical Sunday night in February of 1964.

There are too many choices today diffusing the audience far too much. Even if we got invaded by Neptune, some people would still be tuned in to one of the shopping channels or trying to find a college basketball game that's on somewhere. And that doesn't count those who are glued to their DVD players, X-Boxes, or their phones or the internet. We will never again be a society where we all discover an overnight sensation over the course of the same night.

Of course, in reality, The Beatles weren't overnight sensations. It really took them about seven years. Seven years of some bad performances, bad contracts, bad living conditions before, ultimately, eight minutes of black and white adrenaline set them off on the most phenomenal year anyone in show business ever had...and, probably, the most phenomenal 50 years, too.

We've all heard how important first impressions are. Well, that night of February 9th, 1964, 8:02 PM EST proved it. With those few minutes on stage, The Beatles earned the cachet to walk away from the live stage, to experiment in the studio to make music in ways no one had ever heard before, to explore the use of drugs, to make outrageous public statements, to break apart, to attempt to disabuse the group's accomplishments...together and apart, to make sometimes ridiculous, amateurish, self-indulgent music on their own...and we overlooked it all simply because we fell in love with them as those New York teenagers in the theatre on 53rd Street were screaming.

Their one of a kind, never to be duplicated, world conquering appearance on The Ed Sullivan Show. The Beatles Most Memorable Moment of all.

AFTERWORD...REALLY 1,282 AFTERWORDS:

So, there you have The Beatles 50 Most Memorable Moments. From the start of the band through the rest of their lives. And when you look back on things, as we did here, it shows you what an amazing story it is... almost too remarkable to be true, except that nobody writes fiction this good. So amazing that if you weren't around for it, you might not believe it. Yet, so continually extraordinary, that if you were around for some of it or all of it, you probably took a lot of what The Beatles did for granted... like seeing Superman fly for the 1000th time. So much symmetry to it... John brings in Paul, who brings in George, who brings in Ringo. So much irony...the last album they release is called "Let It Be". The last song on the last album they record is called "The End". None of that planned. Lennon the first one into The Beatles is the first one out. The man who sang so often about the value of life has his ended in the most senseless of ways. McCartney the one who went to any lengths to break The Beatles up wound up going to any lengths to put them back together again. Harrison, the one who for decades wanted nothing to do with The Beatles asking on his deathbed that the band keep working together. Starr, the one whose talents were most quickly dismissed being the one who would make the most substantial music longer than anyone else in the band.

And the question always comes up. "Why was it this set of four guys who would do so much for so long?" Well, certainly, they were four very talented, very engaging, very driven young men whose individual gifts fit matchlessly with each other...The Beatles being the prime example of the whole being greater than the sum of its parts.

But it was obvious that The Beatles reached their audience in a way that few other artists...in any area...ever did. That can be the only reason why they've lasted as long as they have. I think that, at least, in terms of music, where most artists try to reach the hearts of their audience...or some, like Metallica, their nervous systems or some, like Bob Dylan or Paul Simon, try to reach their brains, The Beatles touched our souls.

There was a hopefulness to their music, a reassurance...along with the mix of other emotions, so they wouldn't sound like a quartet of Pollyanna's. Go back and think of all the times the band used words like 'all right' or 'OK' or 'yes' in their songs. With all the uncertainty we face, in the world in general and in our own personal worlds today, The Beatles have been that steadying hand on our shoulder. Telling us to keep going. That things were, in fact, 'getting better'. They were not formally religious, at least, not at first, and yet, George's message would be faith, Paul's would be hope, John's would be love...straight out of 1st Corinthians.

Through things like Bangladesh and Live Aid, they would feed the hungry. Through things like One On One, they would nurse the afflicted. They would preach against materialism, hate and violence. And for tolerance, peace and love. This band, the leader of which would offhandedly claim was bigger than Jesus, may have gotten that idea because they were carrying on so much of his work.

Some people, even some of their peers claimed it was all profit driven. That The Beatles were only in it for the money. If that were the case, they would have never broken up. They would have gone on the road, hating the time spent with one another, but raking in millions (and they wouldn't have been the only rock stars to do so). They would have let EMI put out any packages of their music they wished. They would have allowed their music to sell soap or beer or panty liners. After all, a buck is a buck, right?

No, they understood, early on, that they were not just another rock band. They inspired all of us and, as a result, inspired themselves. They would later on reject everything they preached to us...negate it publicly, walk away from it and each other only to realize how precious it was and ultimately, re-embrace the band and all it stood for. The Beatles became their own prodigal sons.

The last few holdouts might say that The Beatles had the run they've had because they were lucky. Yeah, it was good fortune that Brian Epstein had some acetates cut by a guy who knew George Martin and could set up a meeting. And, yeah, Ed Sullivan witnessing Beatlemania first hand was certainly a stroke of luck. And The Beatles hitting at home just as a government security scandal broke and hitting here as JFK was killed...In fact, their first appearance on American TV...on the CBS Evening News... was scheduled for 11/22/63...was stuff that, obviously, not even the best PR firm could arrange. But, as Branch Rickey once famously said, "Luck is the residue of design". I think he was talking about 'instant karma'.

But luck only lasts so long. At some point, you have to be good. And The Beatles, of course, were much more than good. But, beyond that, The Beatles weren't satisfied with being a good band or a great band...even the best band...or the biggest.

They wanted to sell records...yes. To get that commercial recognition that said the masses appreciated their music. Sure, it would make them rich, but it was much more than that, too. They wanted people to more than enjoy their work. They wanted us to respect it. They wanted their music to stand apart from the other bands in Liverpool, then in England, then in America. They did that, too. But they still weren't satisfied. Ultimately, they wanted their music to mean something. More than change the world, The Beatles wanted to help it. (They wound up doing both.)

Maybe that's not what John was thinking when he put the Black Jacks together in 1957. But it was his obsessive drive...matched by the equally obsessive drives of the other three that made it all happen.

Even on the basis of all that marvelous, incomparable music The Beatles made, I don't think that's why we still honor them so much today. The subtext of all their work...the music, books and films and everything else...that we got from them in ones, twos, threes and fab fours...was how they cared, how they loved and how they worked to make this world better. An amazing agenda for a pop band and, had someone presented it to them somewhere along the way, you couldn't have blamed them if they'd quit right then and there.

If they didn't understand it, well, we sensed it from the start. That's why we grabbed on to them in 1964. Wouldn't let them go after 1970 and drew them closer still to us as they locked arms in the "Real Love" video.

You can understand why they chose "Love" as the title of the performance art overview of their years together done by Cirque De Soleil. That's what they shared. That's what they spread. And that's what they wanted us to spread.

As a result of that, The Beatles, over the last 50 years haven't given us 50 memorable moments, they've given us a million of them. And, I have no doubt there will be many, many more to come.

About Casey Piotrowski

There may be other people who know more about The Beatles (probably). There may be others who have more experience in radio (doubtful). But nobody brings to the table the equal measure of both of those essentials as Casey Piotrowski...and those talents combined to create an arc of radio shows, which led to the publication of Casey's first book..."The Beatles 50 Most Memorable Moments".

Before he could drive a car, he was playing records on the radio. Before he graduated from college, he was getting fan mail from Europe...a result of working on a 50,000 watt station on the East Coast. His radio stops included Buffalo, Cincinnati, the Bay Area and Southern California. Top rated and well-remembered, Piotrowski was twice nominated by Billboard for its "Air Personality Of The Year" Award in two different catagories. He released an album's worth of his on-air comedy and offered a subscription humor service.

And he branched out from there. He's written for network TV ("WKRP in Cincinnati"), appeared on network TV (including, Fox's "Firefly"), in films (including "The Longest Shadow" which was screened at Cannes), done national voice work and appeared on stage and in national and international commercials. He's written and directed a pilot for The 'B' Movie Channel ("Kinkert & Flatstead Pick The Flicks") and is the process of producing his first feature film.

As for the connection to The Beatles, he'd hear them on the radio in early 1964, watched their debut at his Aunt Jenny's house, understood that rock and roll had been revived and became one of the faithful.

While in Cincinnati, he led an on-air campaign that netted thousands and thousands of signatures to help John Lennon get his green card. He worked as a technical advisor to the film, "John Lennon: Imagine" and was a long time contributor to the 'Lost Lennon Tapes' radio series on Westwood One. And he led a world wide effort to get The Beatles a "Record Of The Year" Grammy for the group's last new release, "Real Love". And, since 2002, he has hosted and produced the nationally syndicated radio series, "The Beatles Show"...and written it, too...to the tune of over 2,250,000 words...more than anyone else has written on the group.

He has also written on The Beatles for "Goldmine", "Beatlefan", "Record Convention News" and other rock publications. And has broken a number of world-wide broadcast exclusives about the band's work through the years. He has also authored three e-books on the band, "Readle The Beatles". "The Beatles Show's Second E-Book" and "1 + 1 + 1 Is 3".

And it is all those CD's, books and magazine articles and stray pieces of knowledge that have gathered through the years coming together with that wide range of experience... as a performer, as a writer...that makes Casey Piotrowski uniquely suited to write that most unique history of that most unique band, "The Beatles 50 Most Memorable Moments".

THE BEATLES: PRESS REPORTS
By: W. Fraser Sandercombe

"You could say I've come to terms with my own nose . . . I have a laugh, and it goes, er, up one nostril and out the other." — Ringo

They captured the hearts of a generation. The whole English-speaking world knew the names John, Paul, George and Ringo. Now you can relive the lives and careers of the Beatles as seen through the popular British music publications of the 1960s.

The Beatles received more media attention than any other rock band in history. This book explores their year-by-year exploits as they grew from a local phenomenon to international superstars. Included are many personal interviews with the Beatles. You will see that their vibrant, honest personalities were just as important to us as their music.

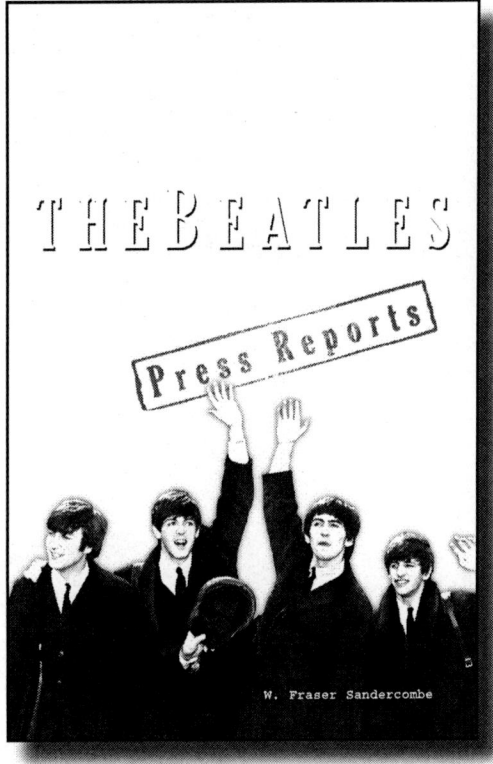

"They're four very different people who get together to form a unit that is virtually impregnable . . . They're very close indeed. A lot closer than people think." — George Martin

From the Cavern Club to their conquest of America, the Beatles were the leading wave of the "British Invasion," and they set the standards for the music world. The Beatles: The Press Reports is more than a trip down memory lane; it is the history of the Beatles as witnessed by the insiders of the British press

ISBN 978-1-894959-61-2
$23.95 CDN
$19.95 USD
£11.95 UK
Visit www.cgpublishing.com for more information

The Beatles Christmas Book

by Belmo and Garry Marsh

The Beatles Christmas Book tells for the first time the complete history of The Beatles and Christmas. Within this book you'll learn about the rare Fan Club flexis, the Beatles Christmas concerts, the BBC Radio Specials, rare memorabilia and much more. All presented by Beatles historian and expert Scott "Belmo" Belmer and co-author Garry Marsh.

ISBN 978-1-926592-25-1

$27.95 USD/CDN

Visit www.cgpublishing.com for more information